Marty Noble's
peaceful world

Skyhorse Publishing books may be purchased in bulk at special discounts for sales promotion, corporate gifts, fund-raising, or educational purposes. Special editions can also be created to specifications. For details, contact the Special Sales Department, Skyhorse Publishing, 307 West 36th Street, 11th Floor, New York, NY 10018 or info@skyhorsepublishing.com.

Skyhorse® and Skyhorse Publishing® are registered trademarks of Skyhorse Publishing, Inc.®, a Delaware corporation.

Visit our website at www.skyhorsepublishing.com.

10 9 8 7 6 5 4 3 2

Library of Congress Cataloging-in-Publication Data is available on file.

Cover design by Brian Peterson
Cover illustration by Marty Noble

ISBN: 978-1-5107-1036-8

Printed in the United States of America

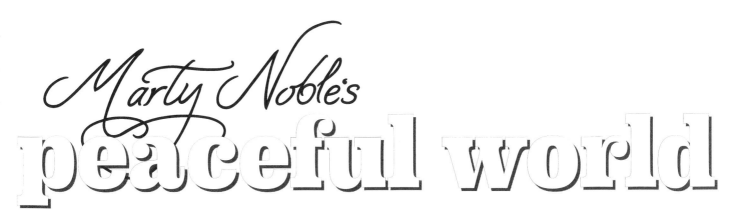

Marty Noble's **peaceful world**

New York Times Bestselling Artist's Adult Coloring Books

MARTY NOBLE

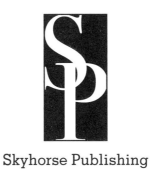

Skyhorse Publishing

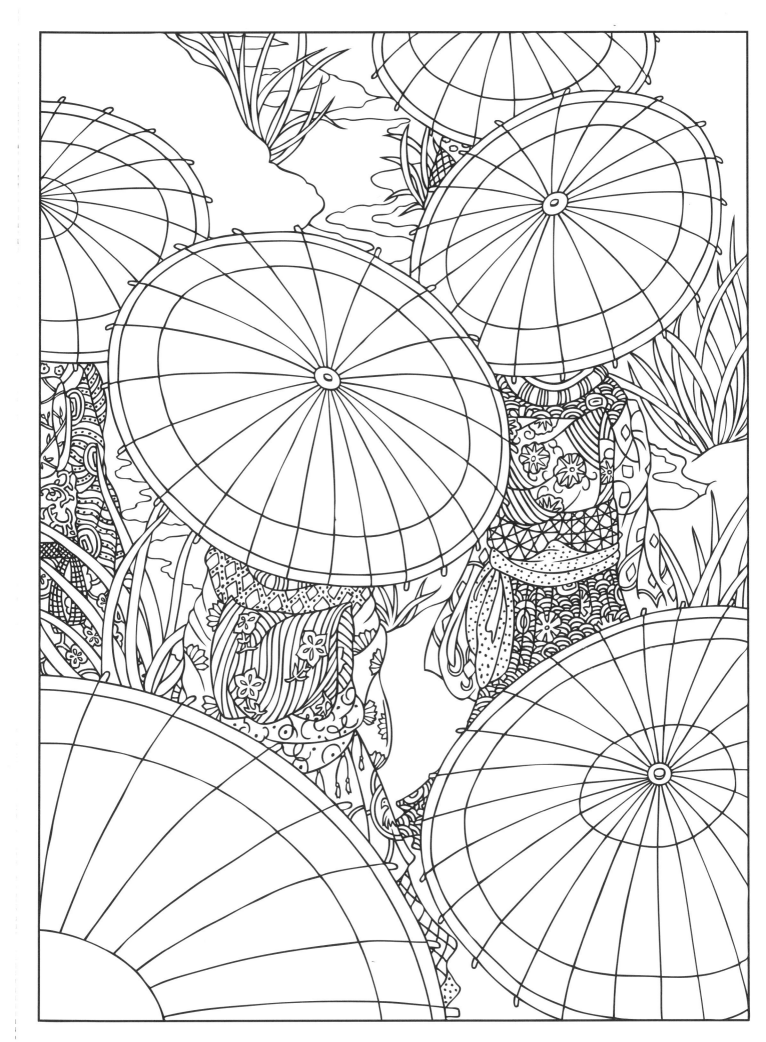

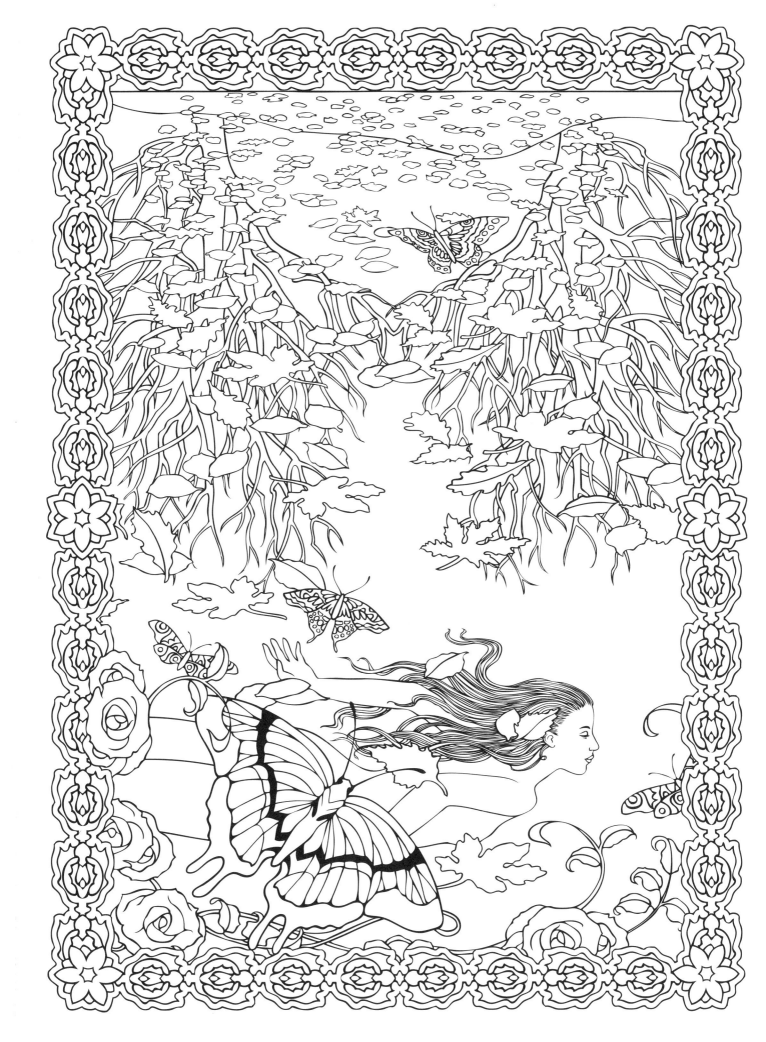

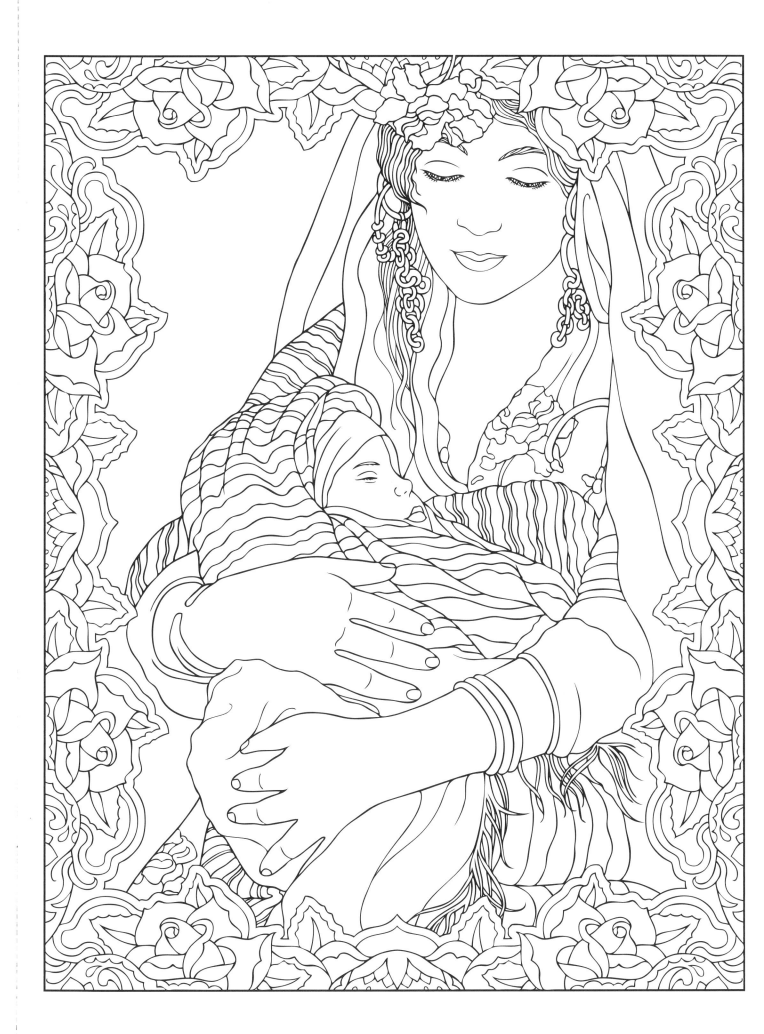

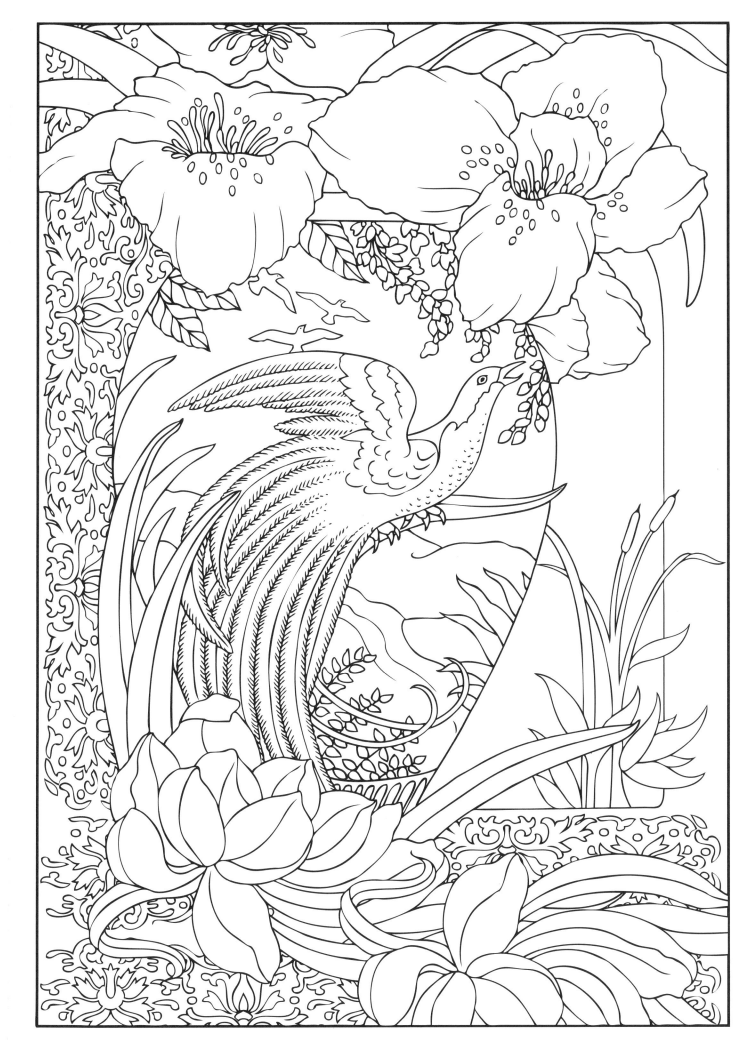

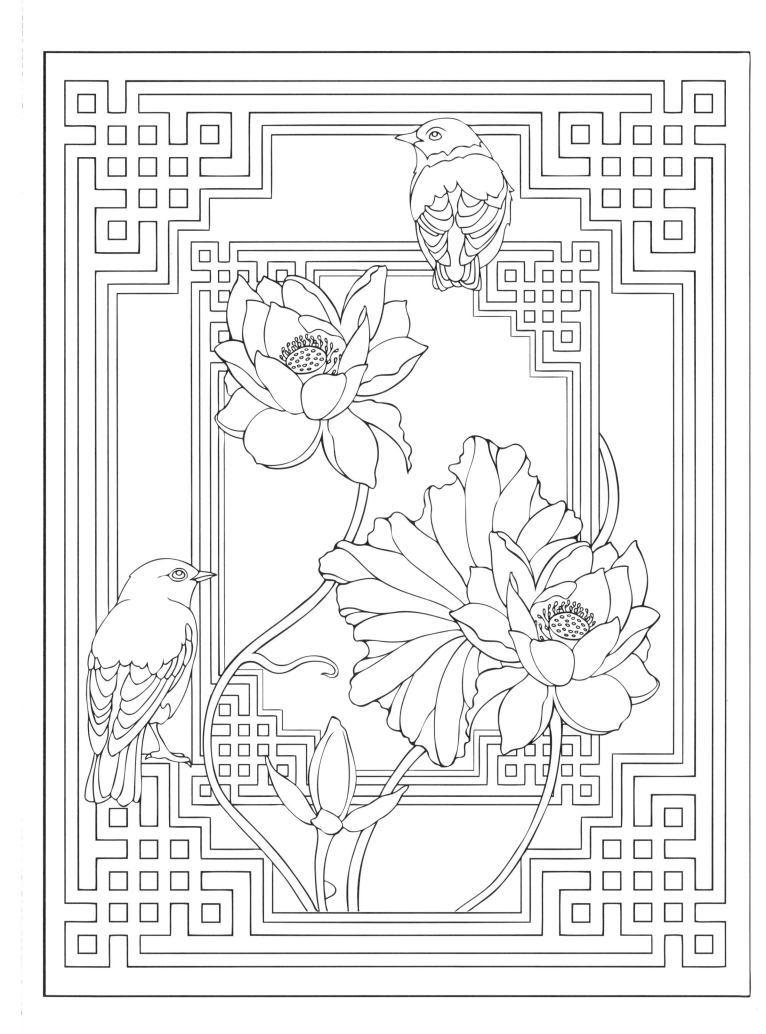

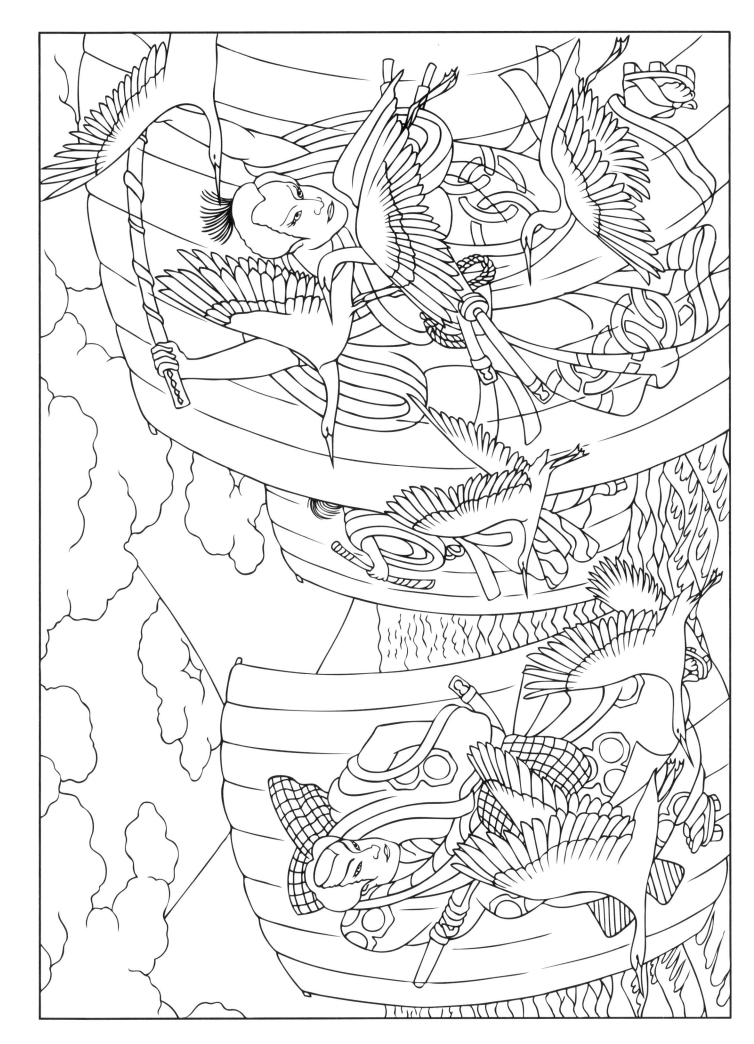

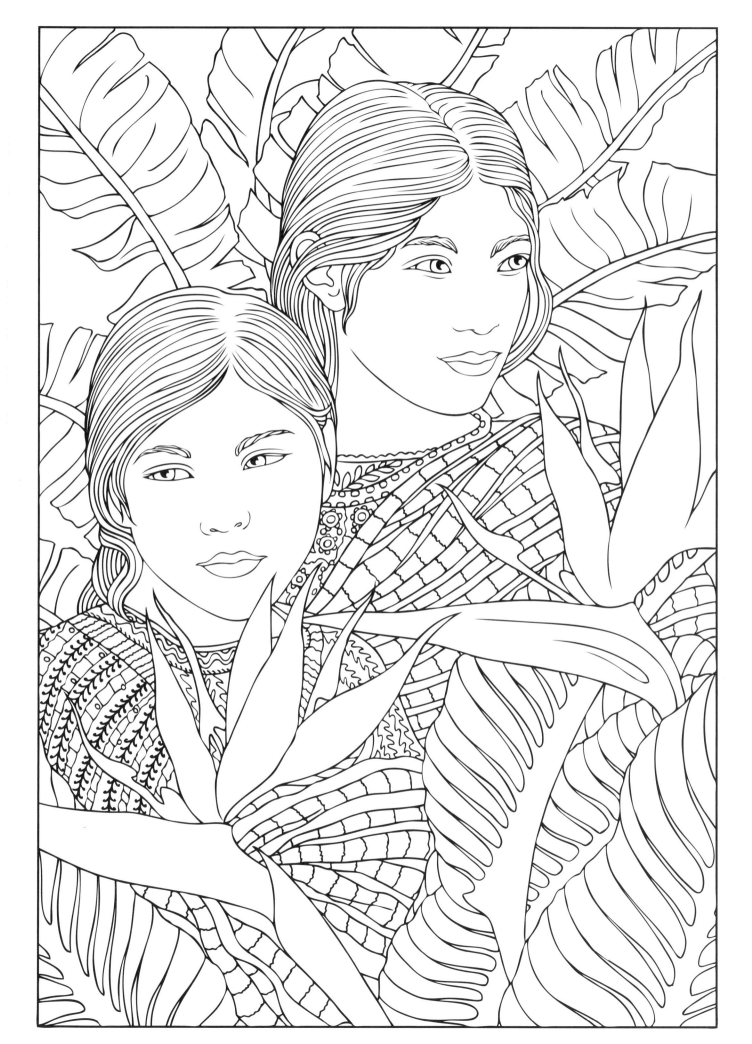

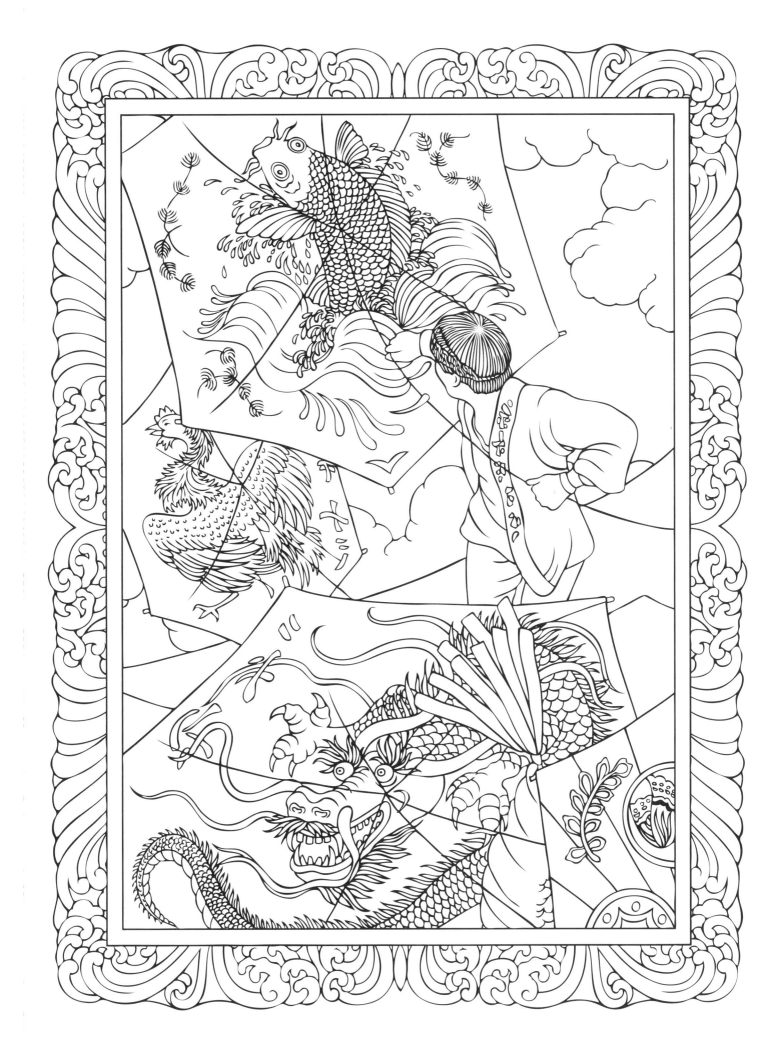

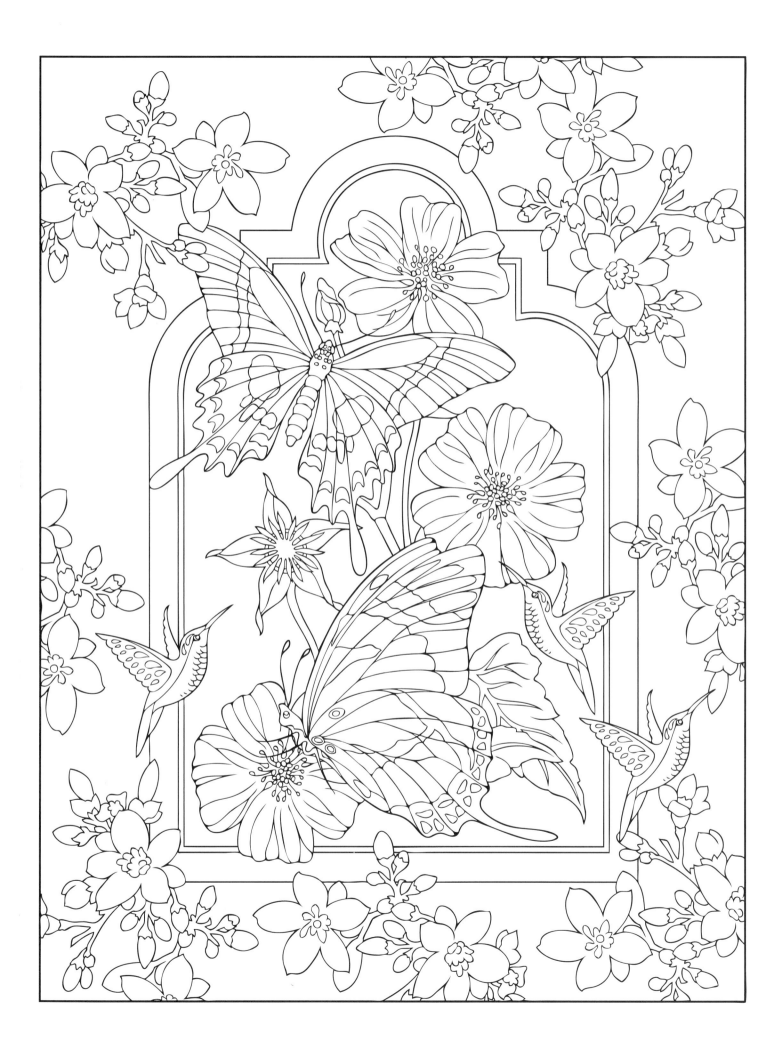

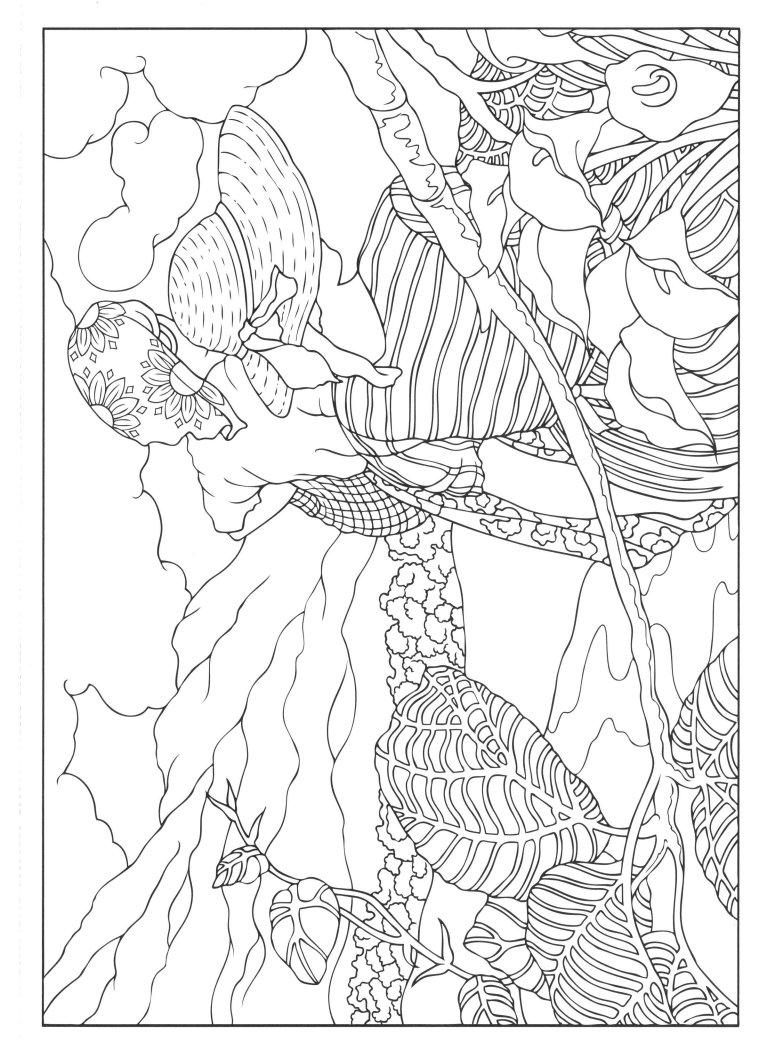

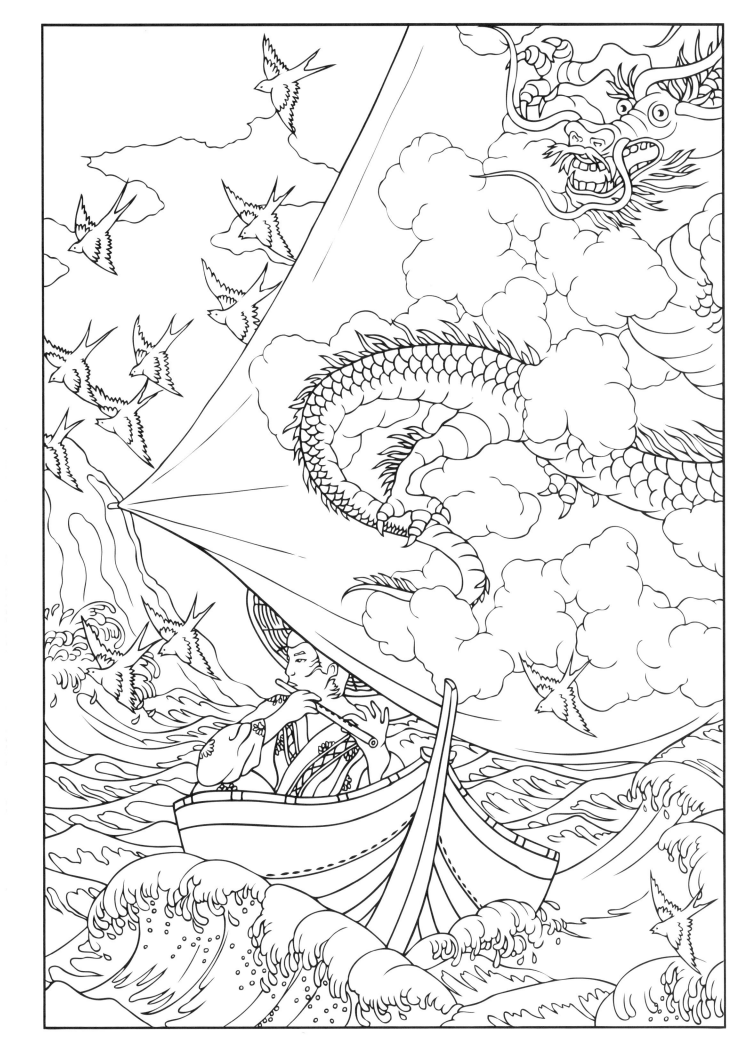

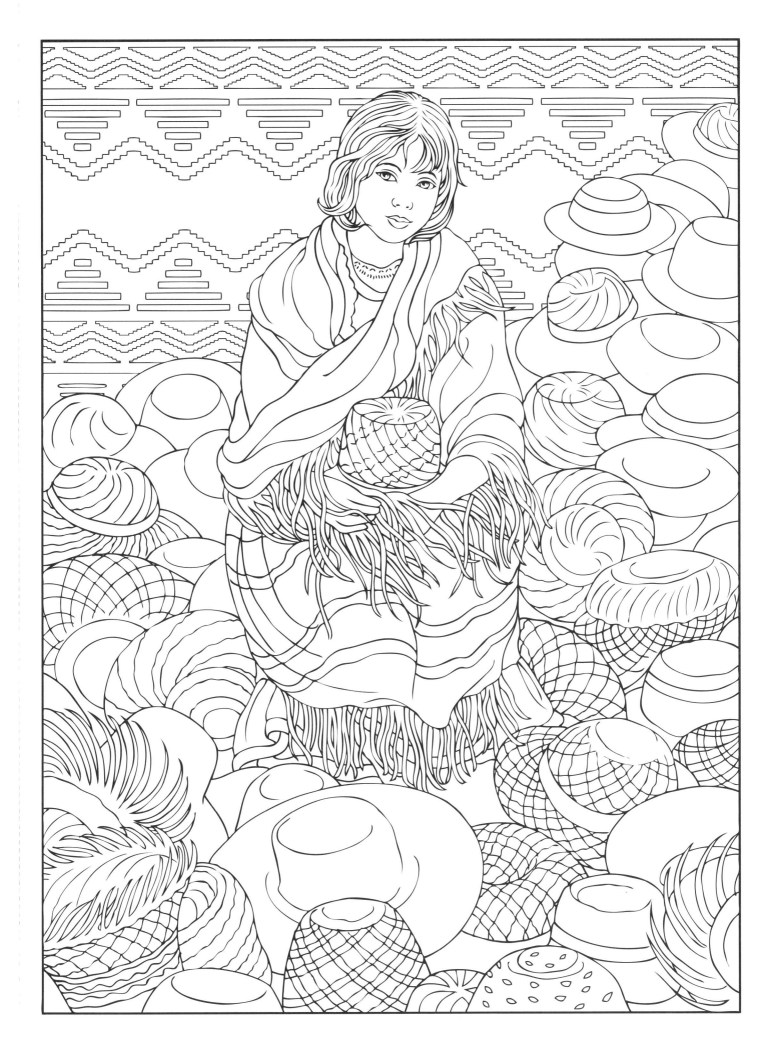

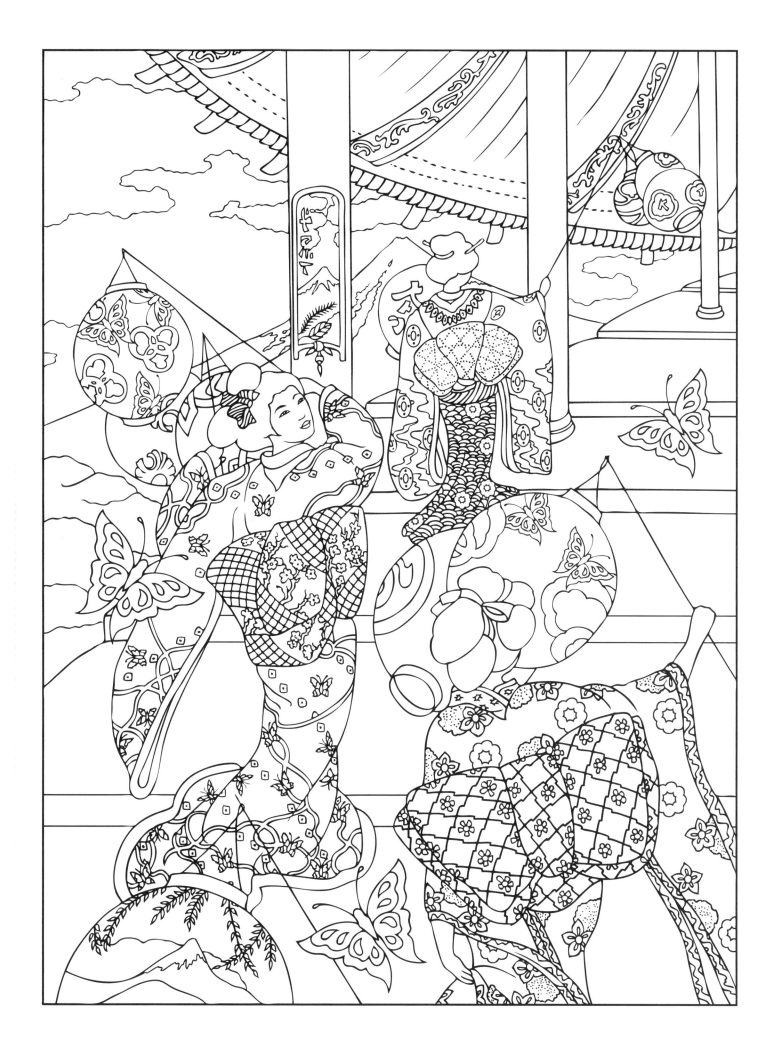

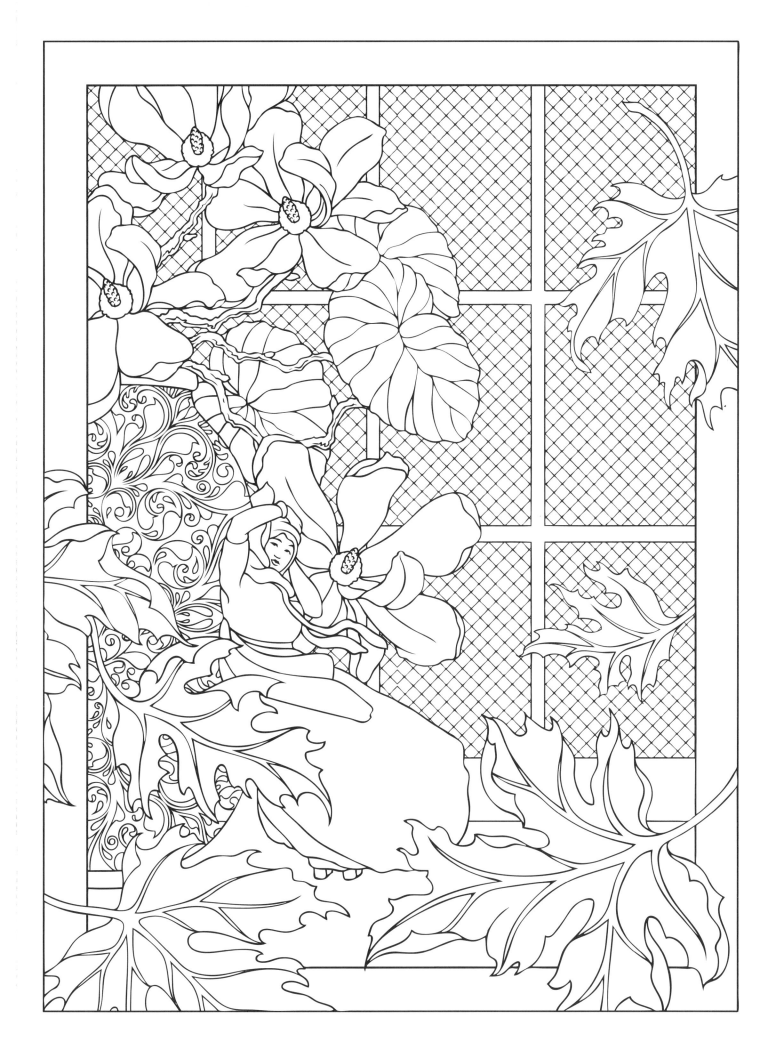

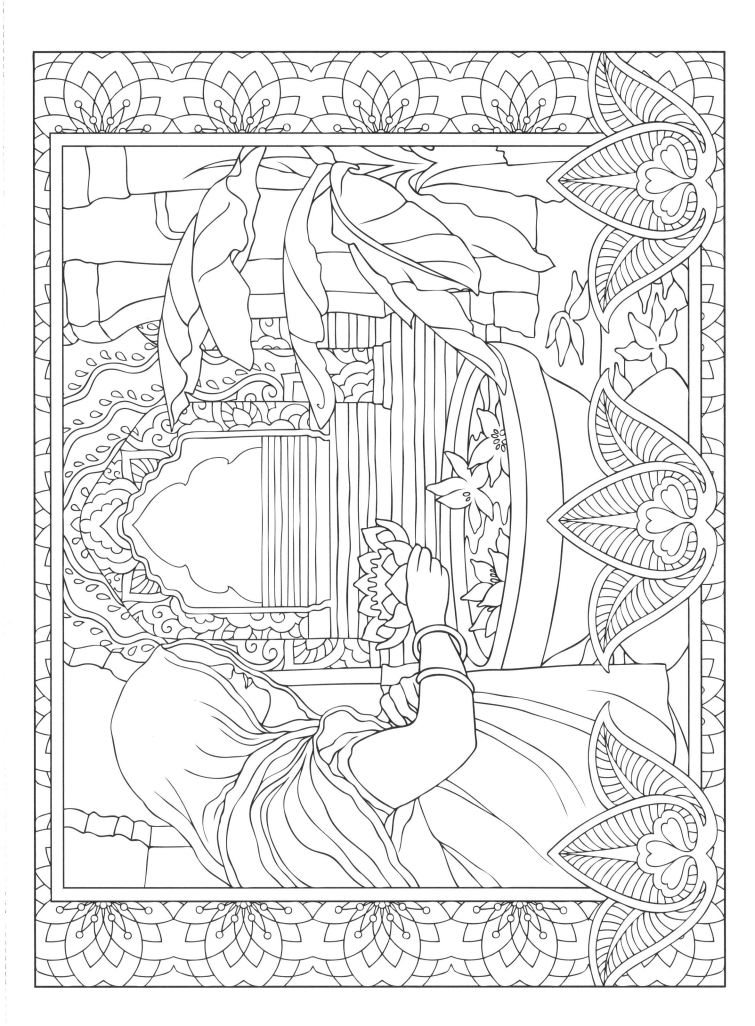

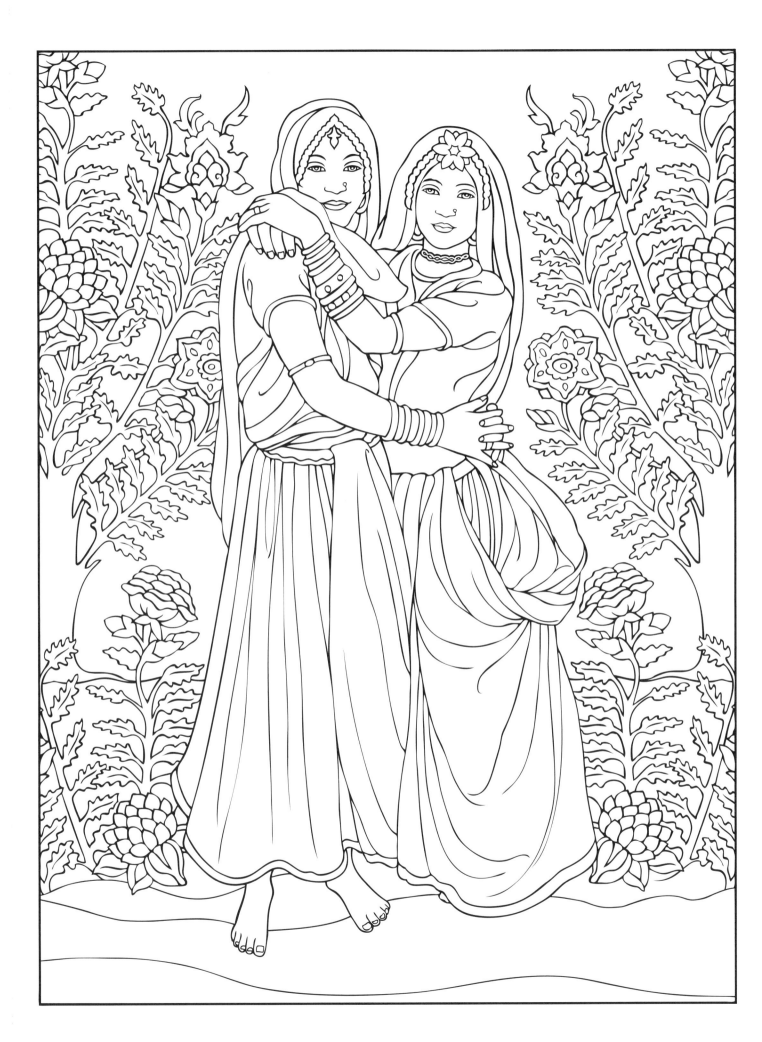

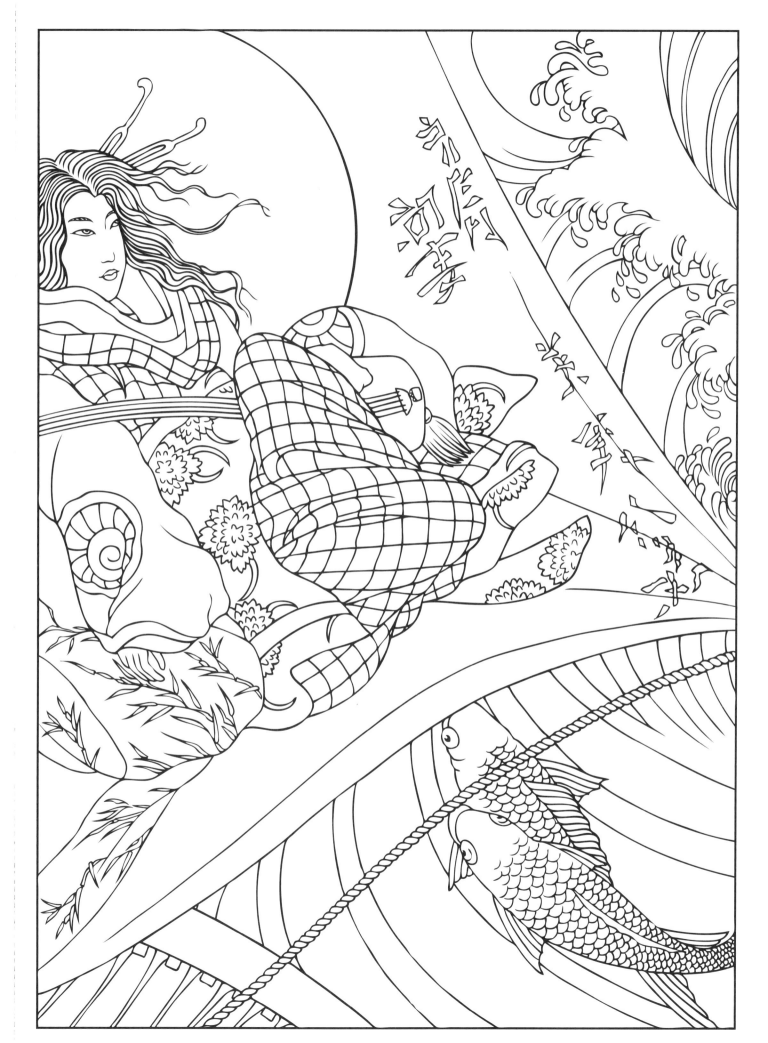

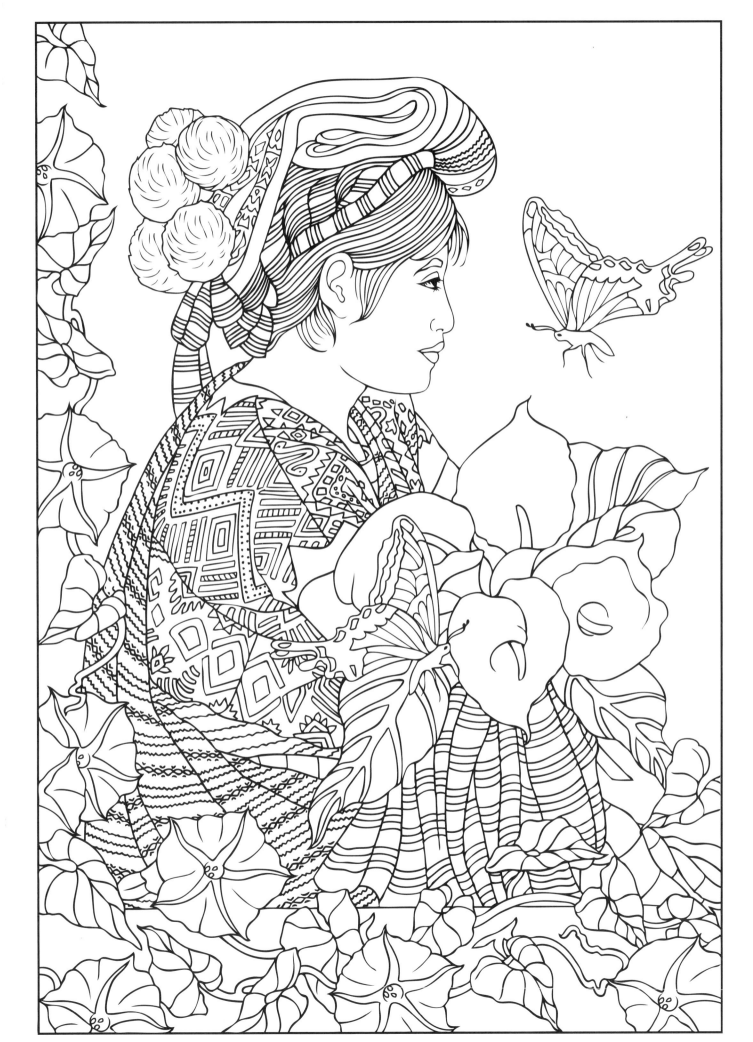

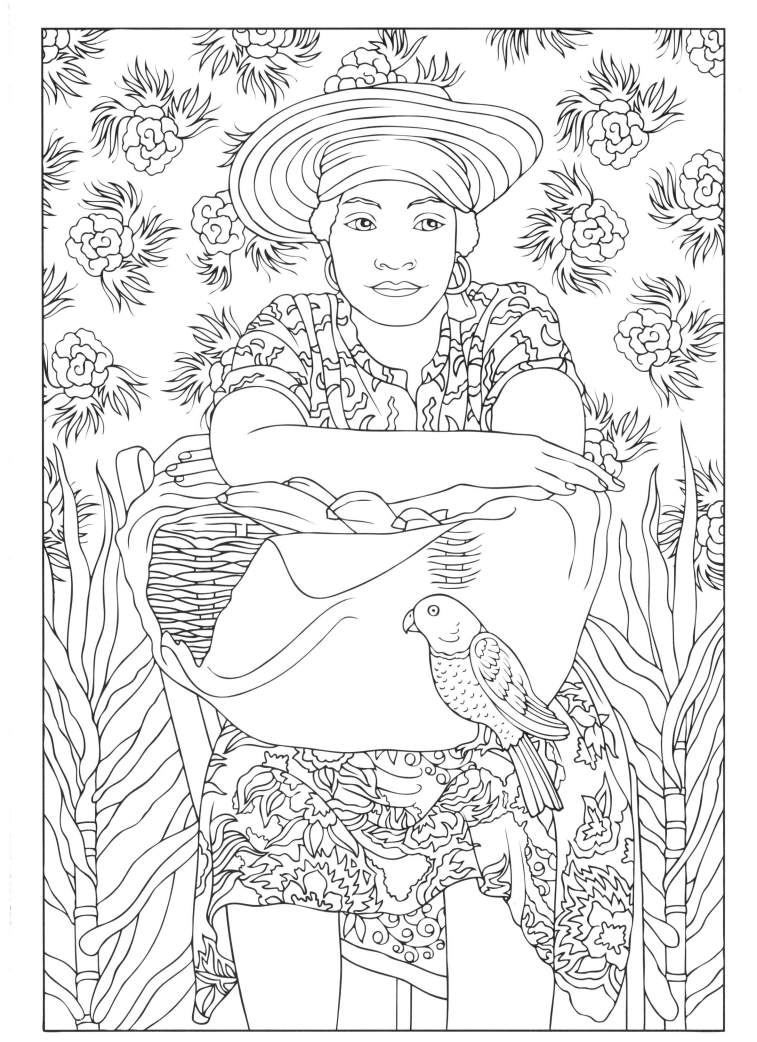

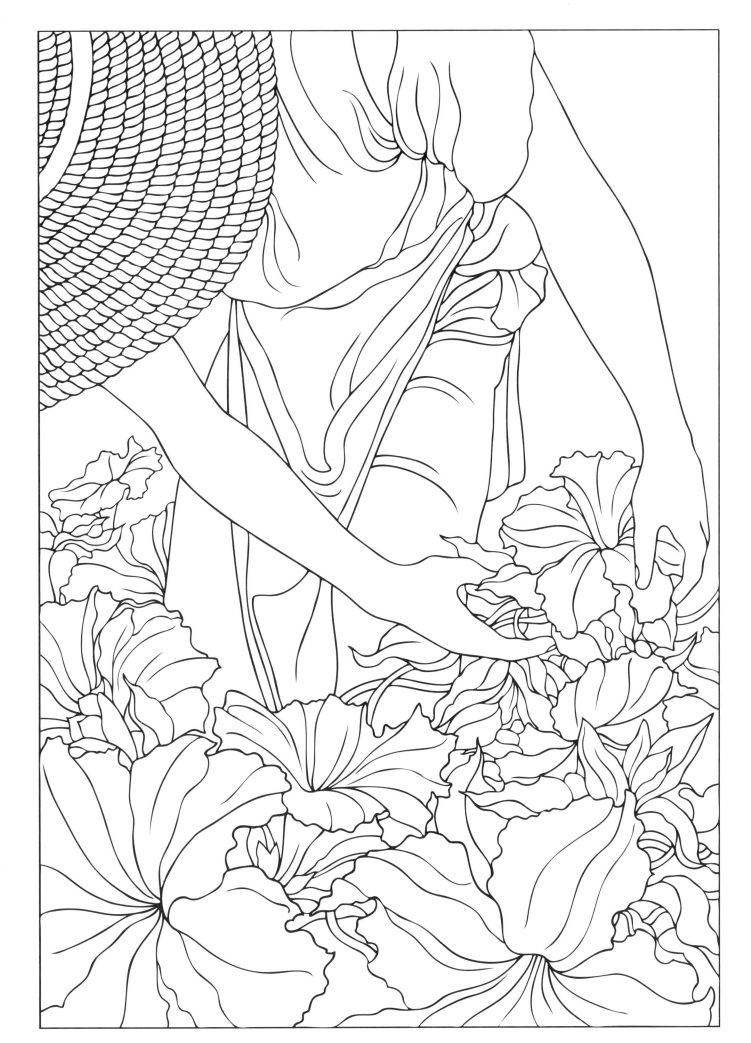

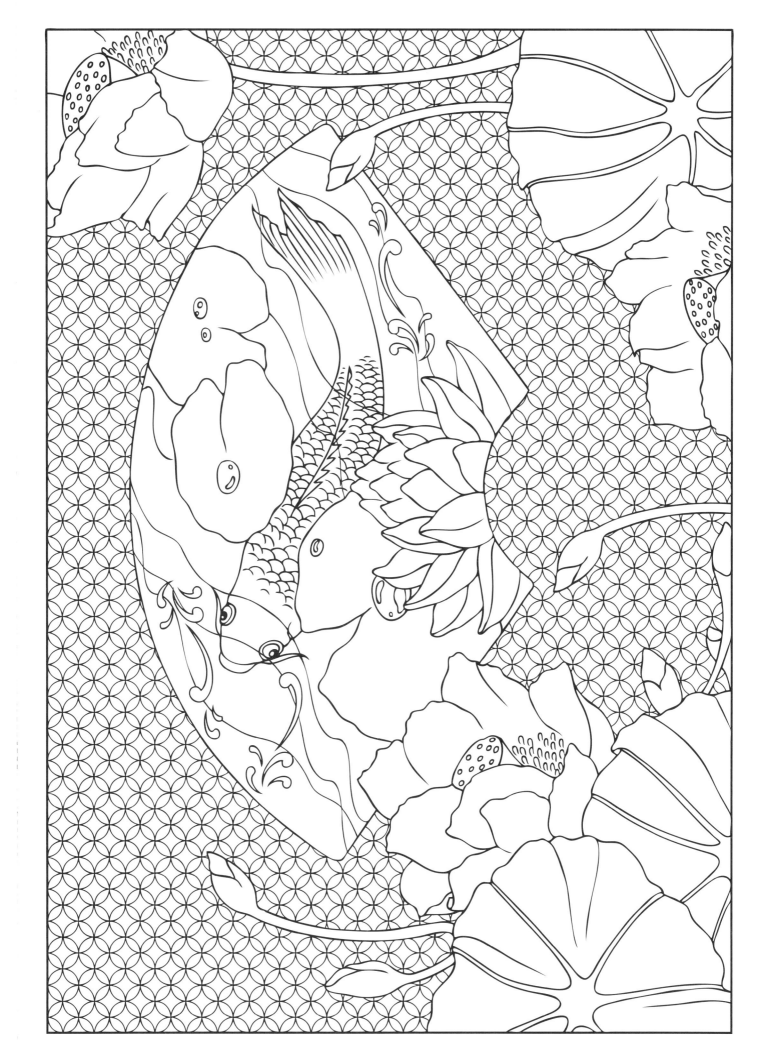

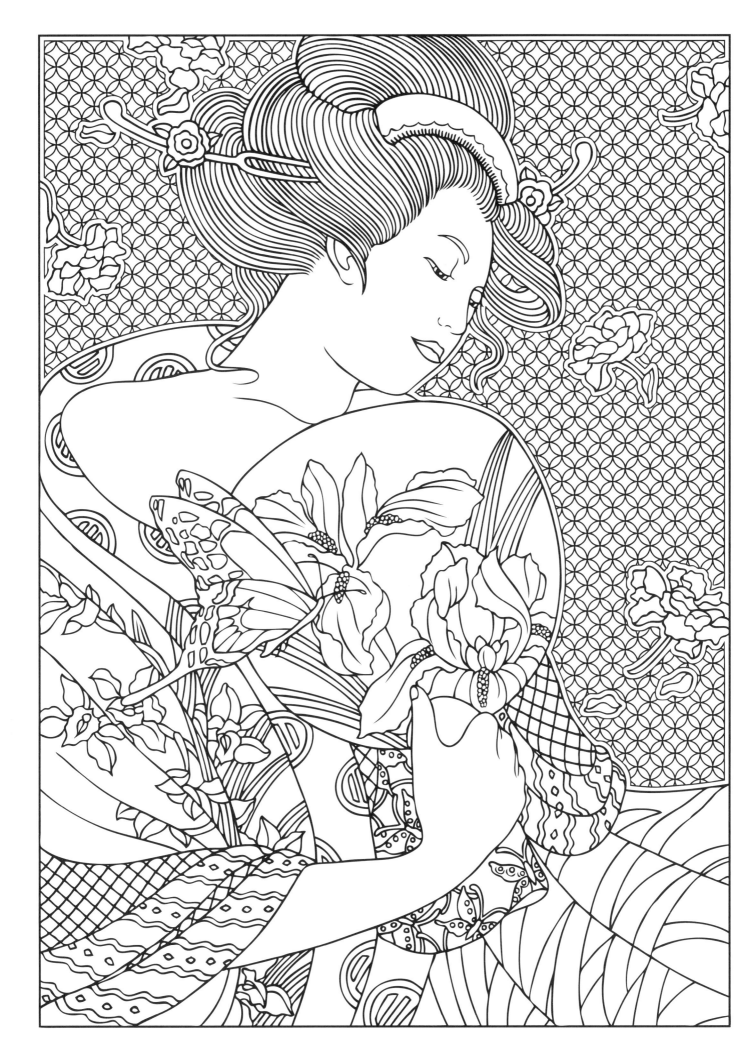

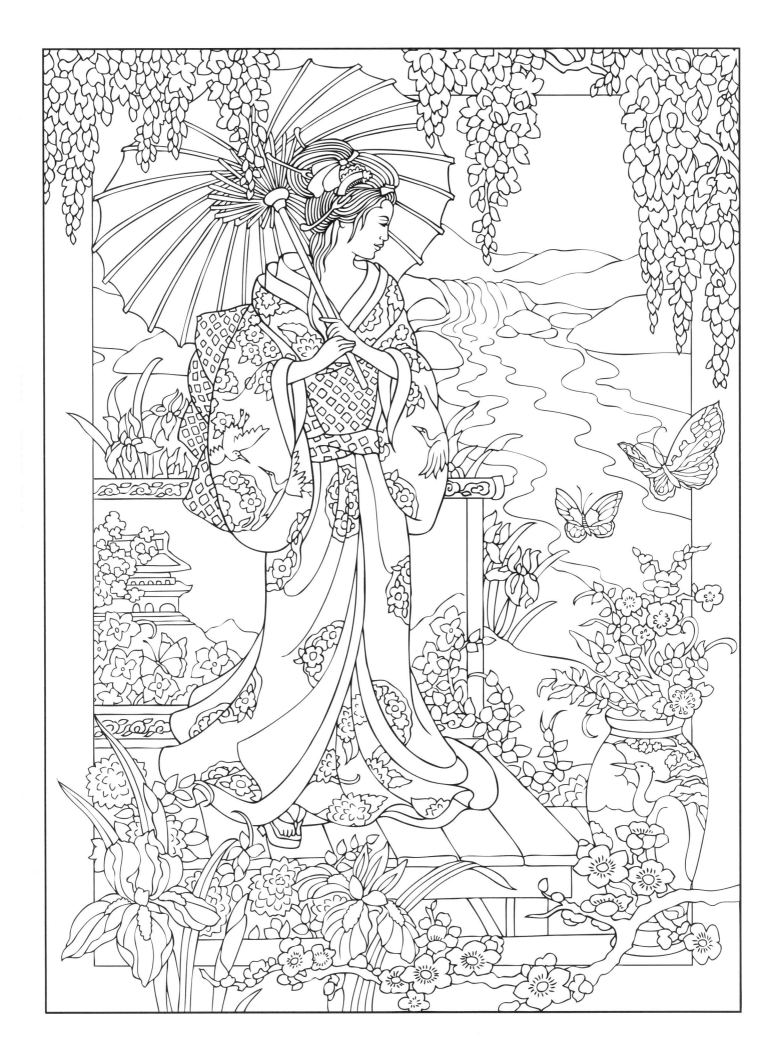

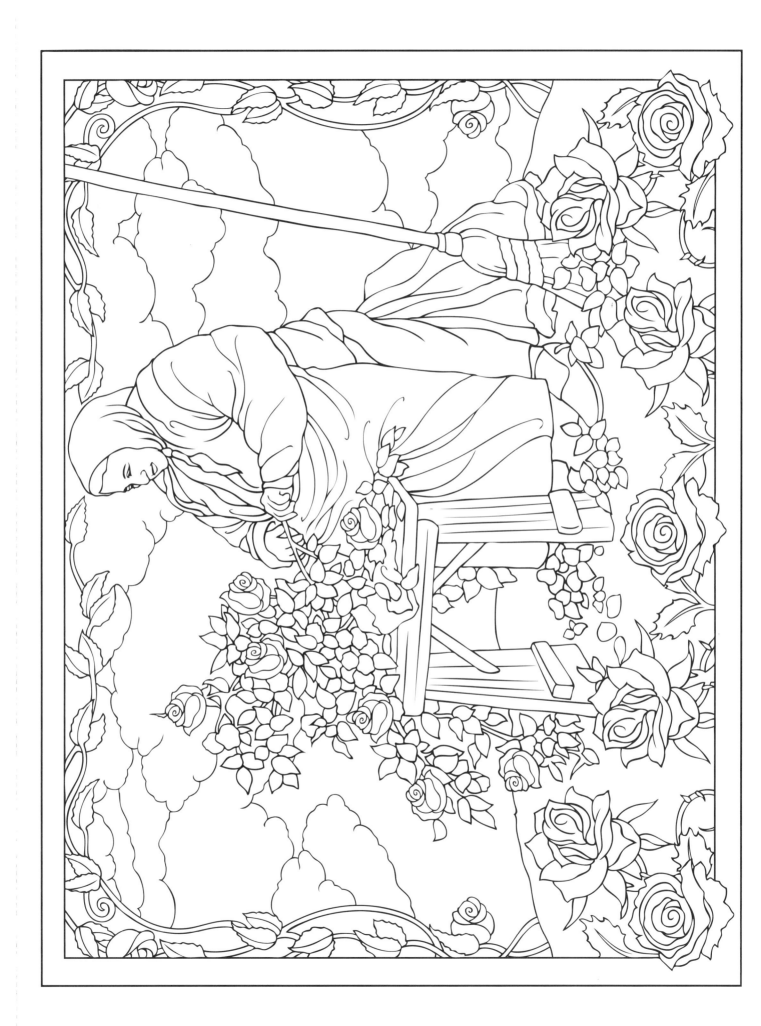

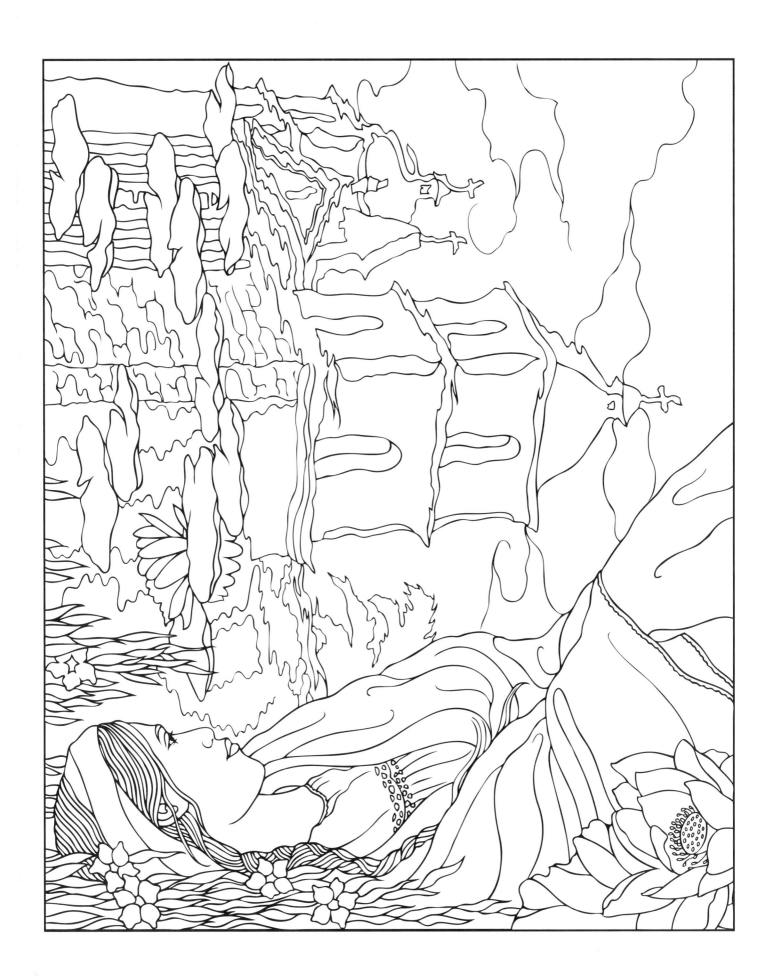

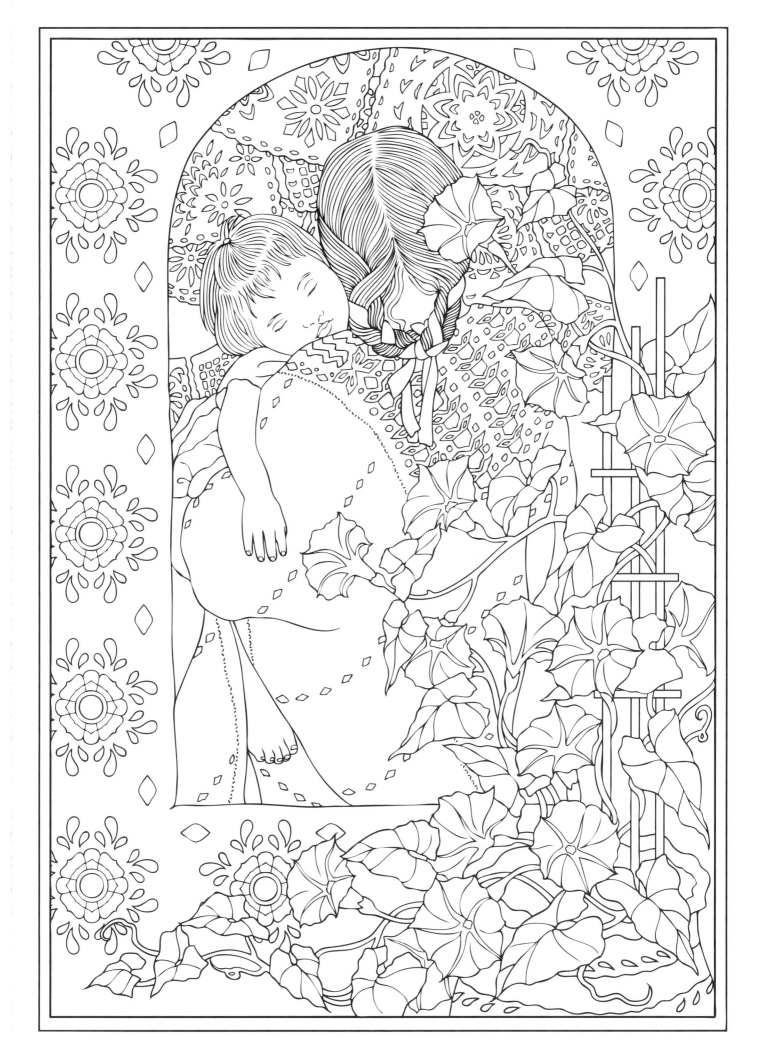

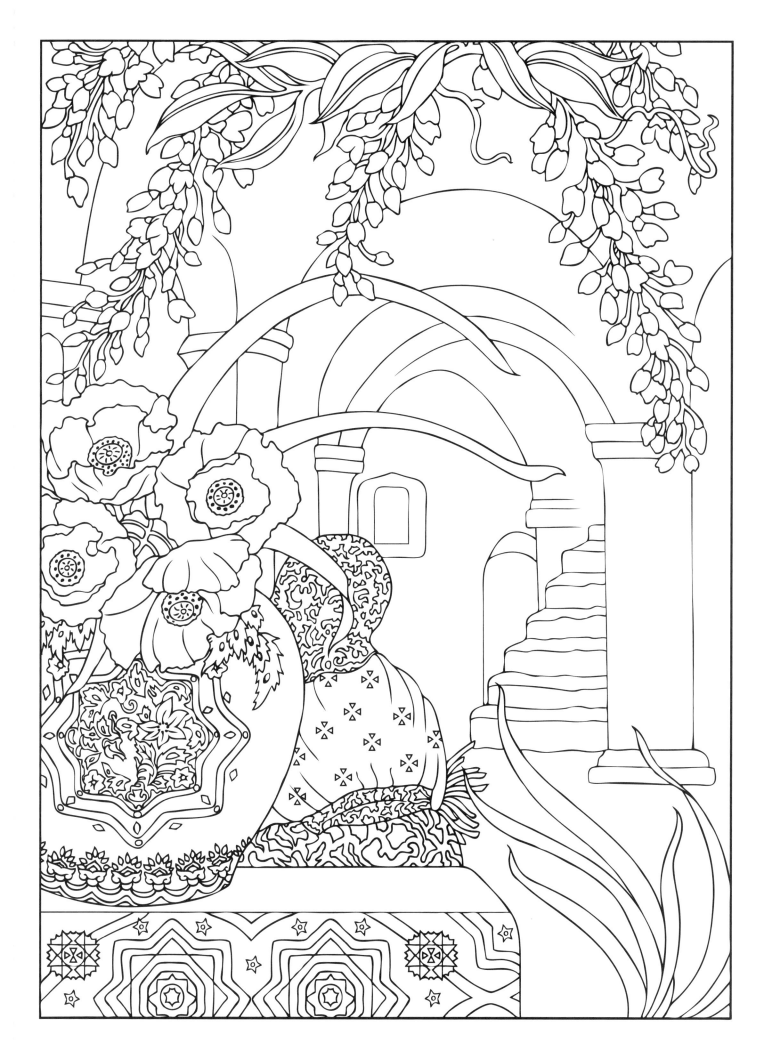

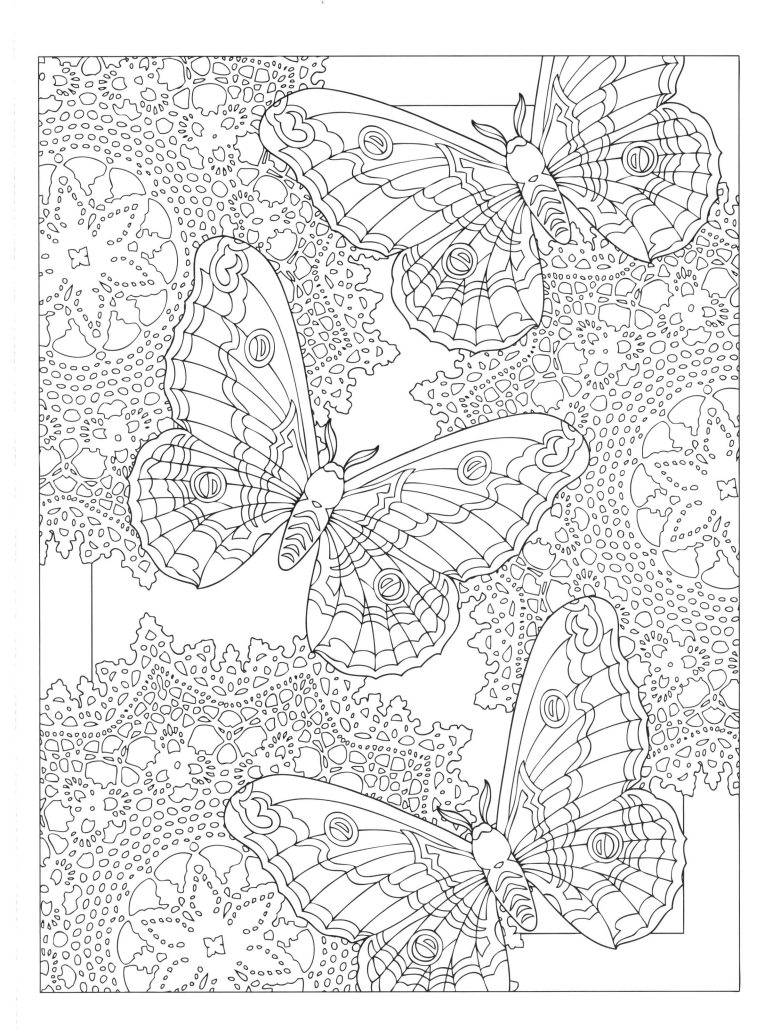

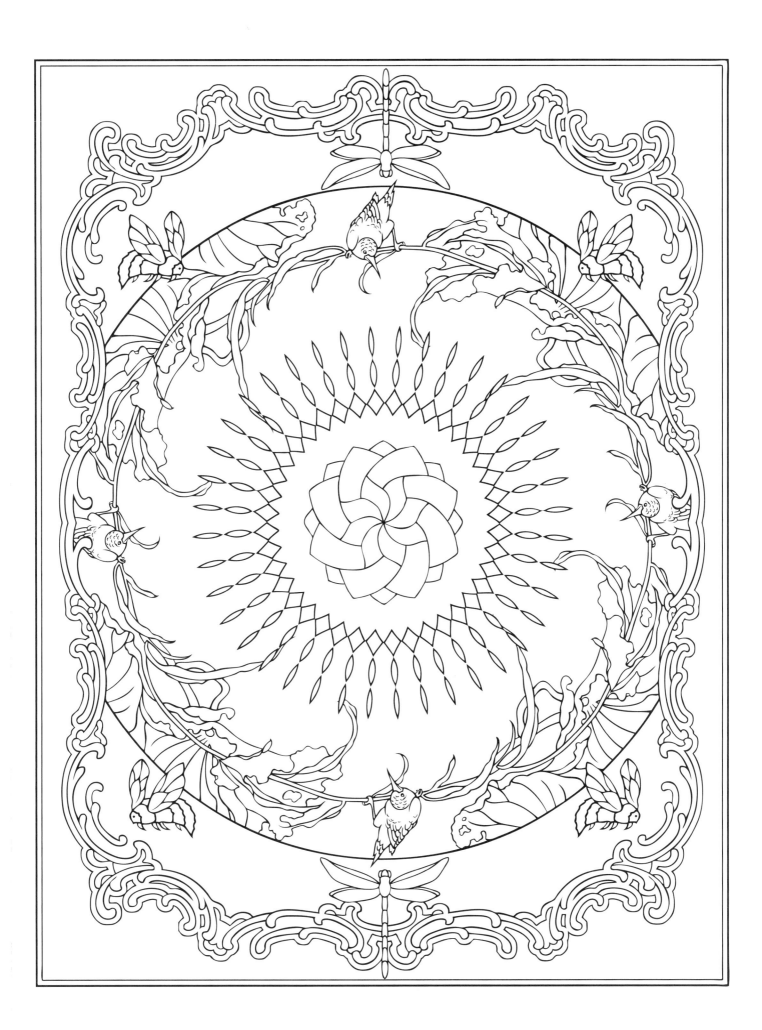

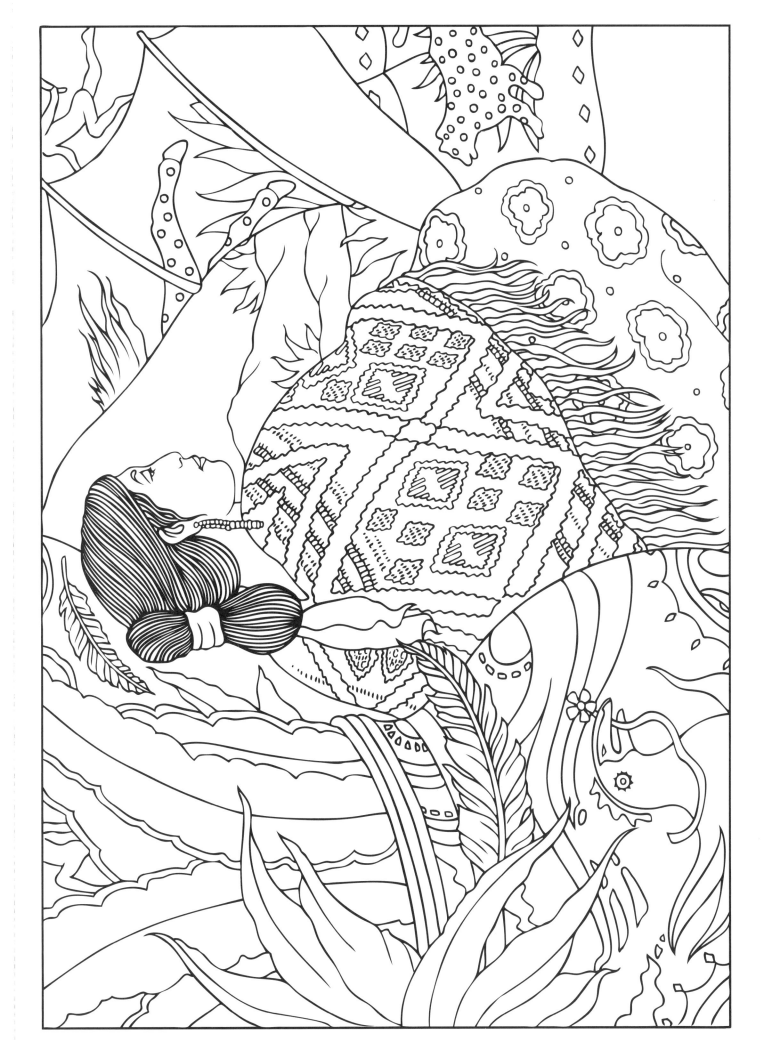

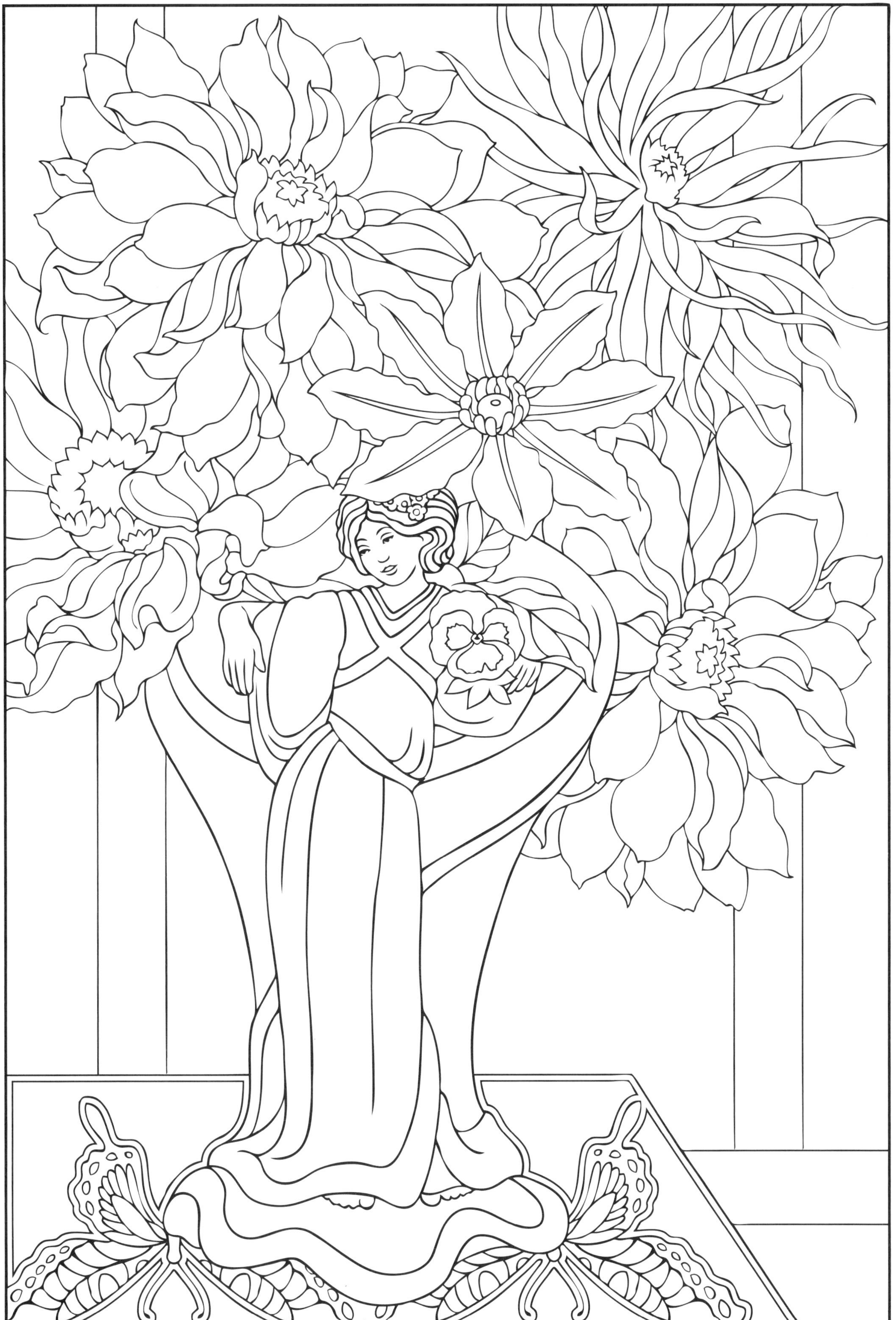

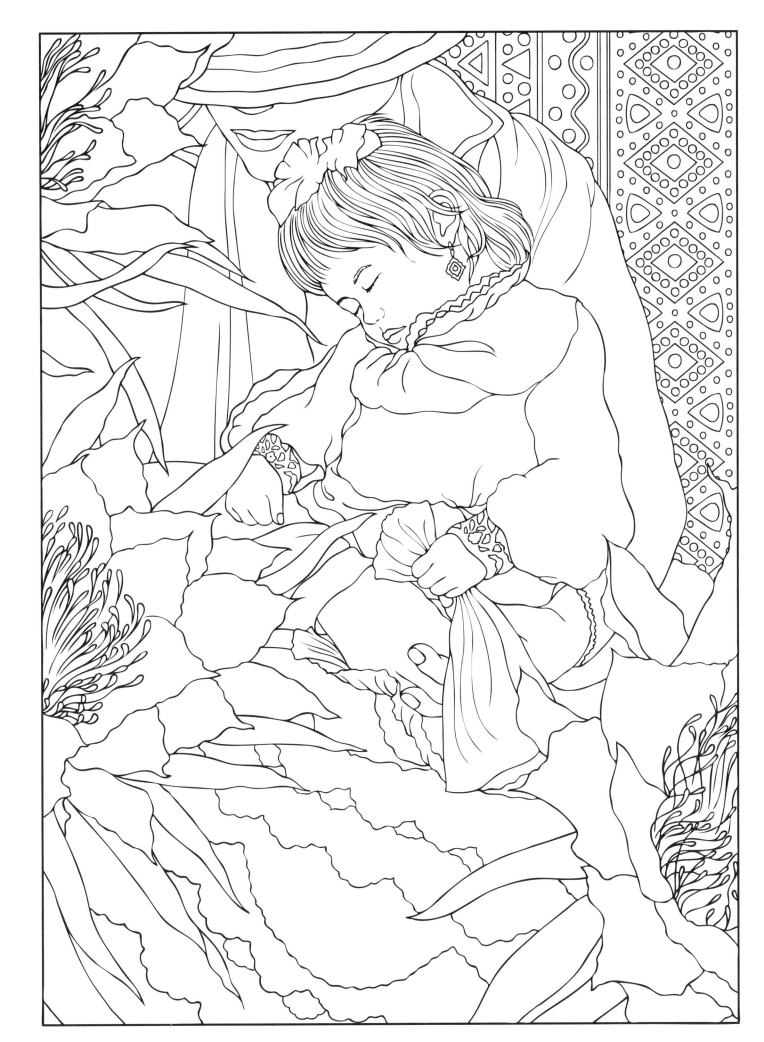

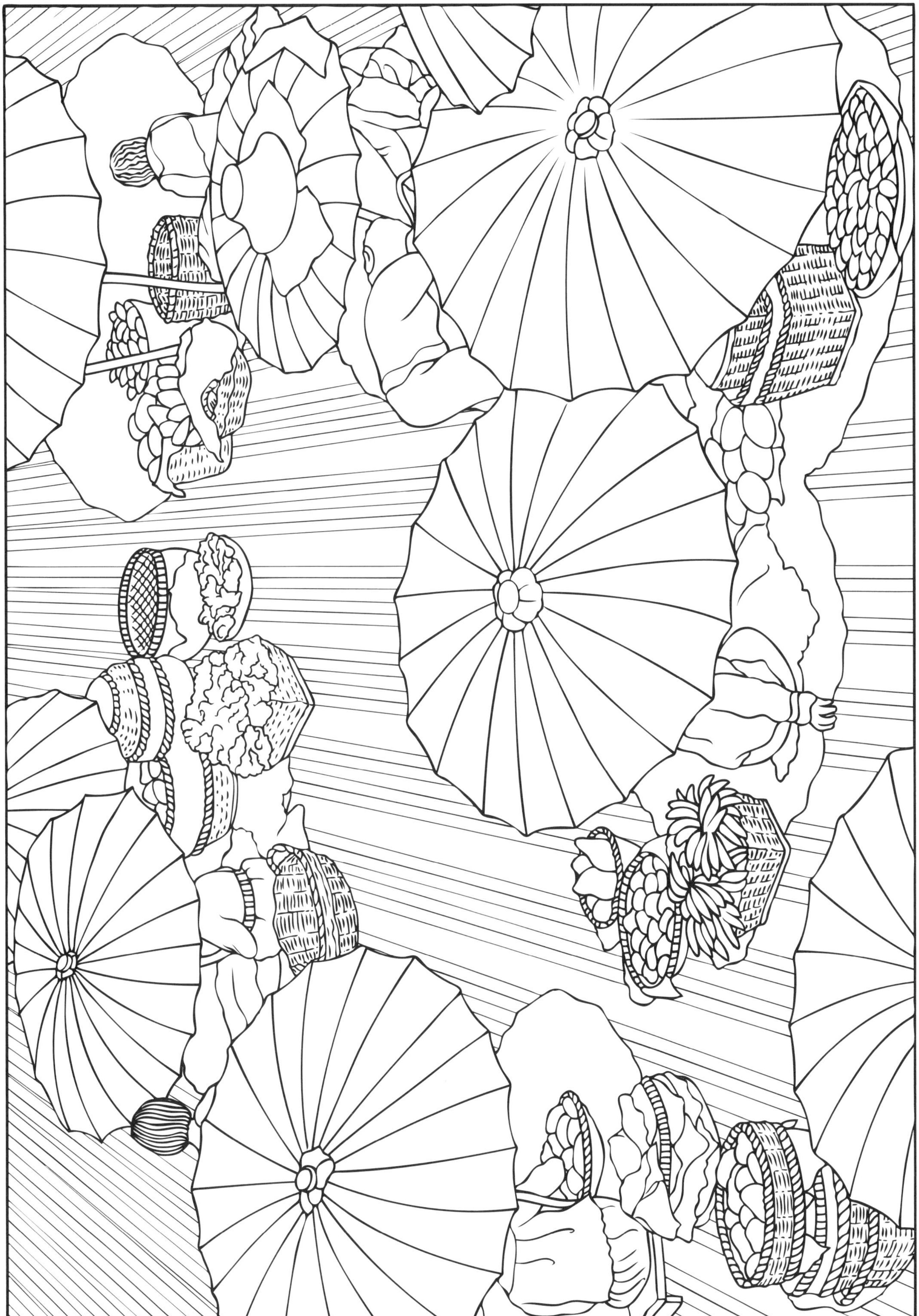

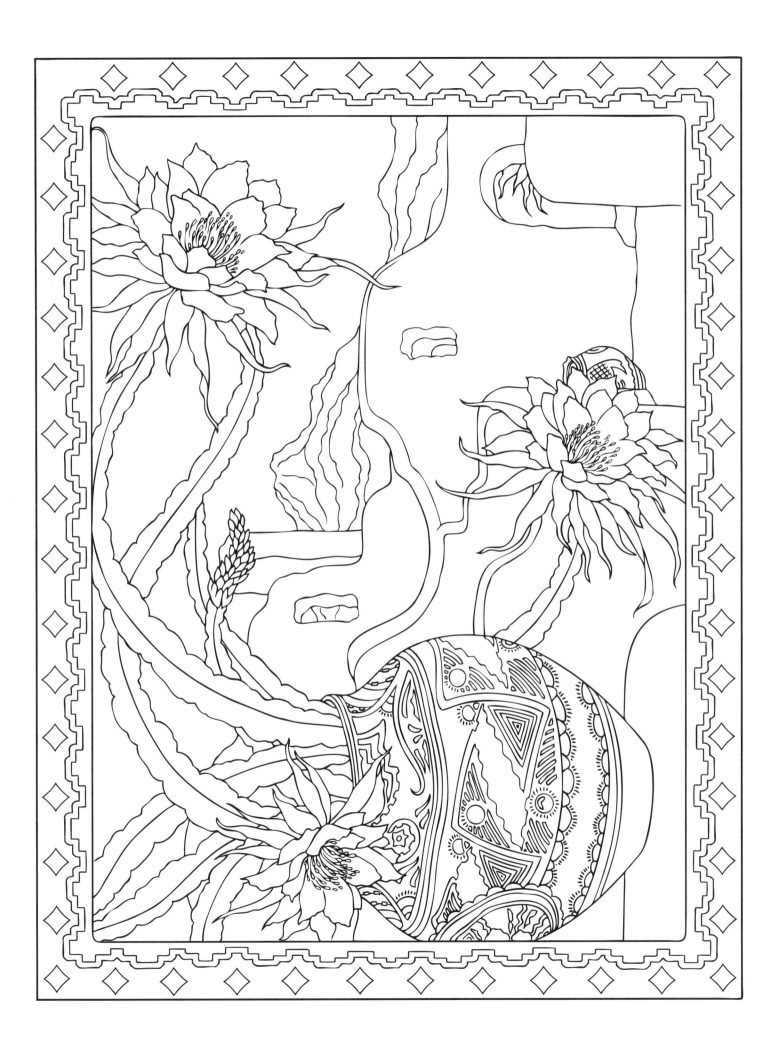

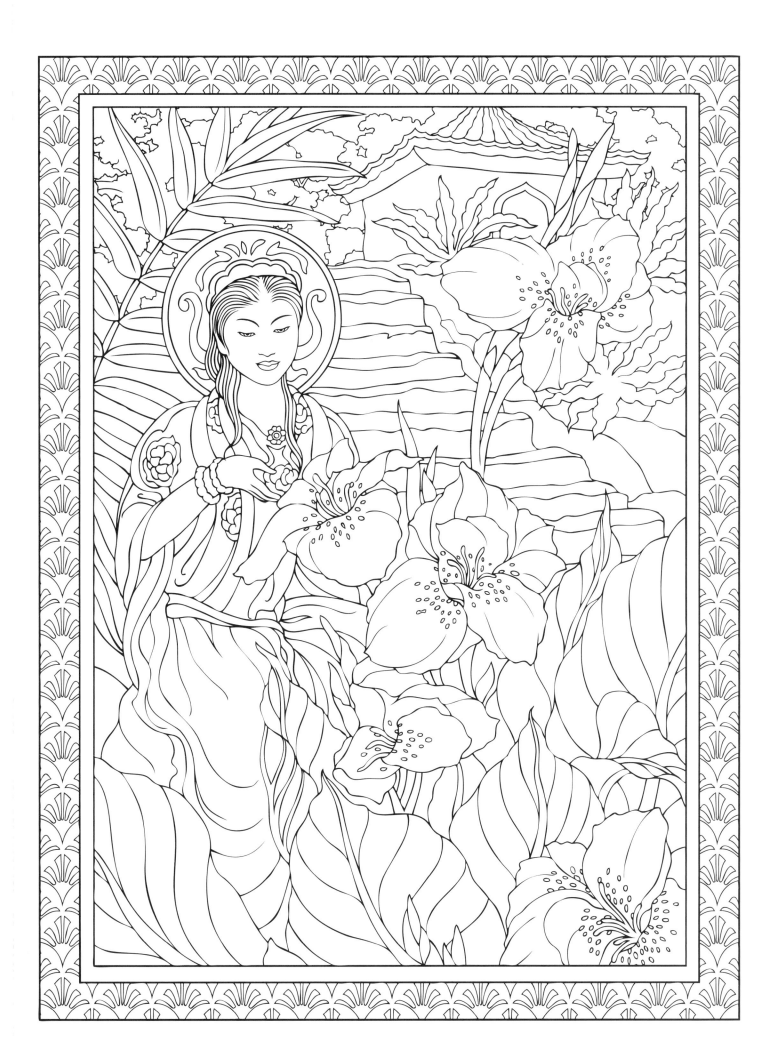

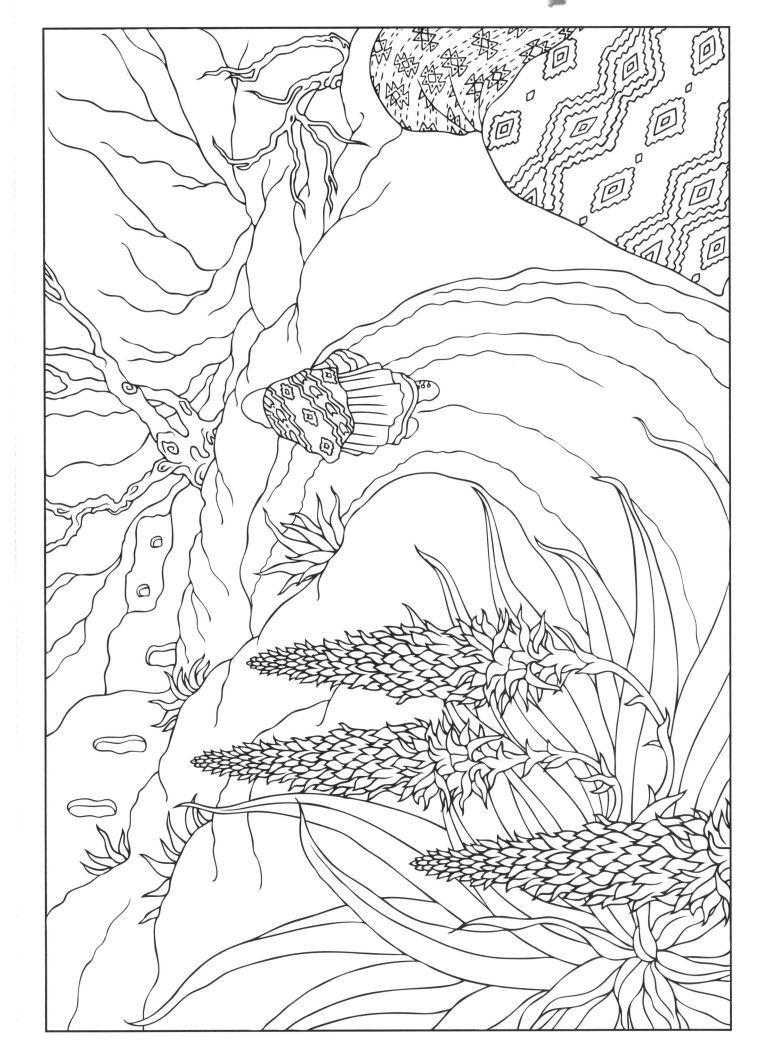

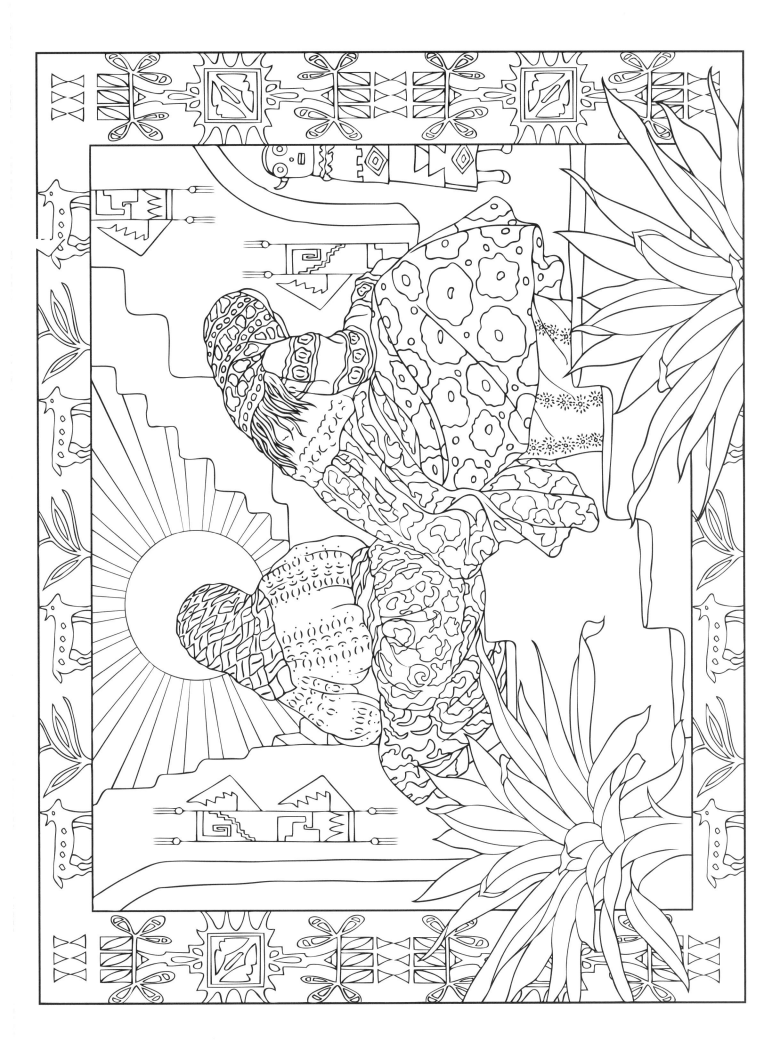

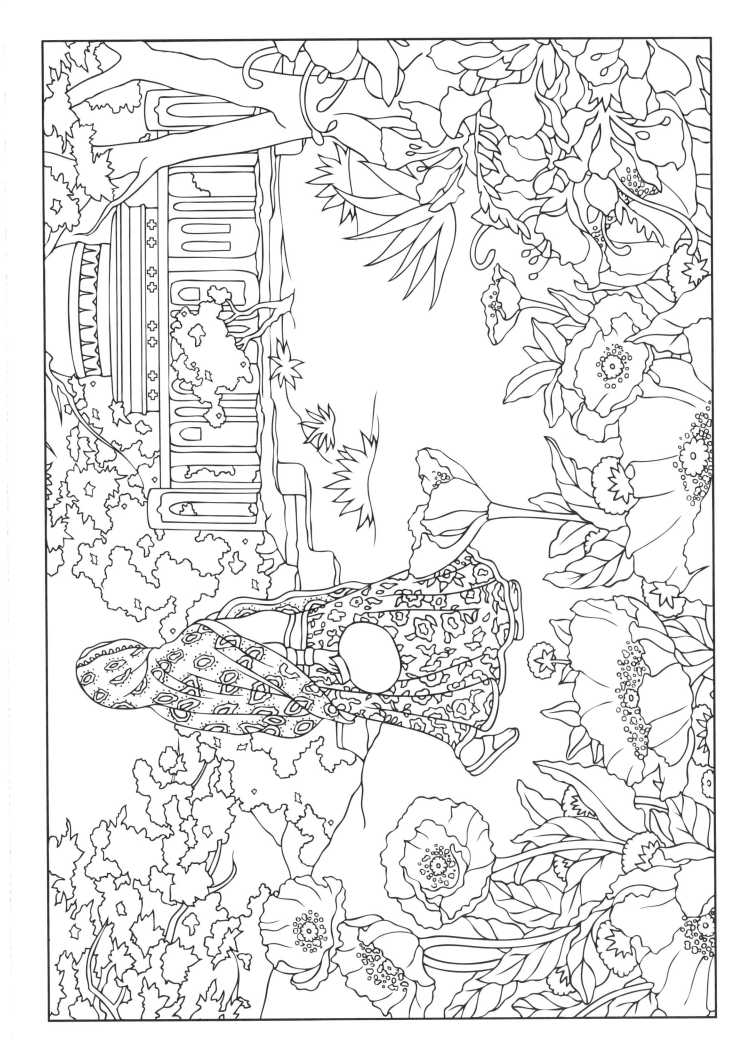

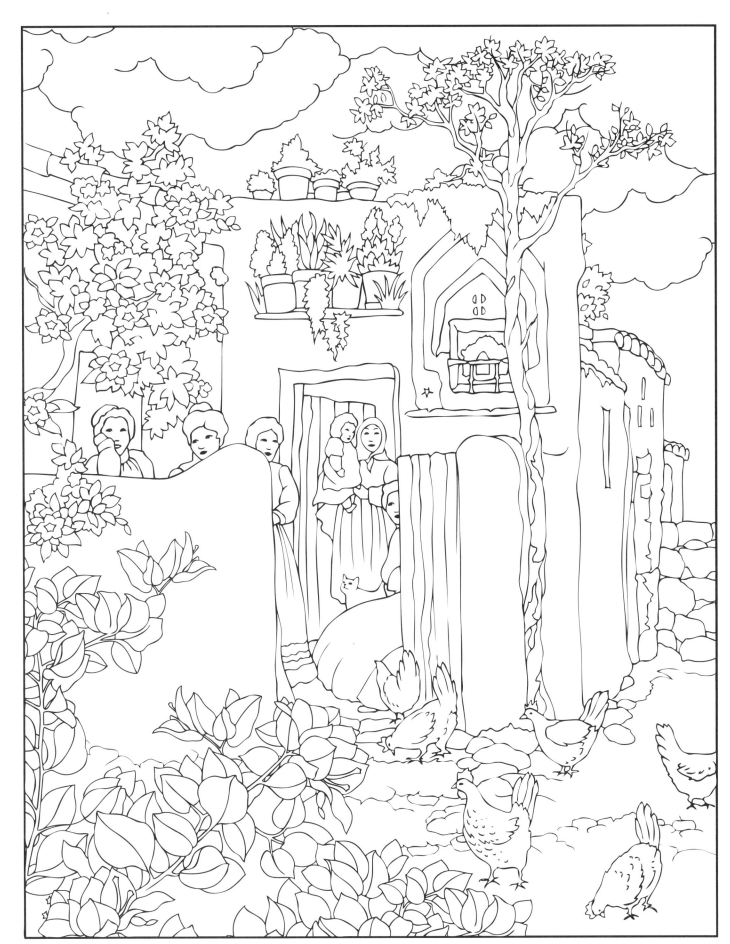

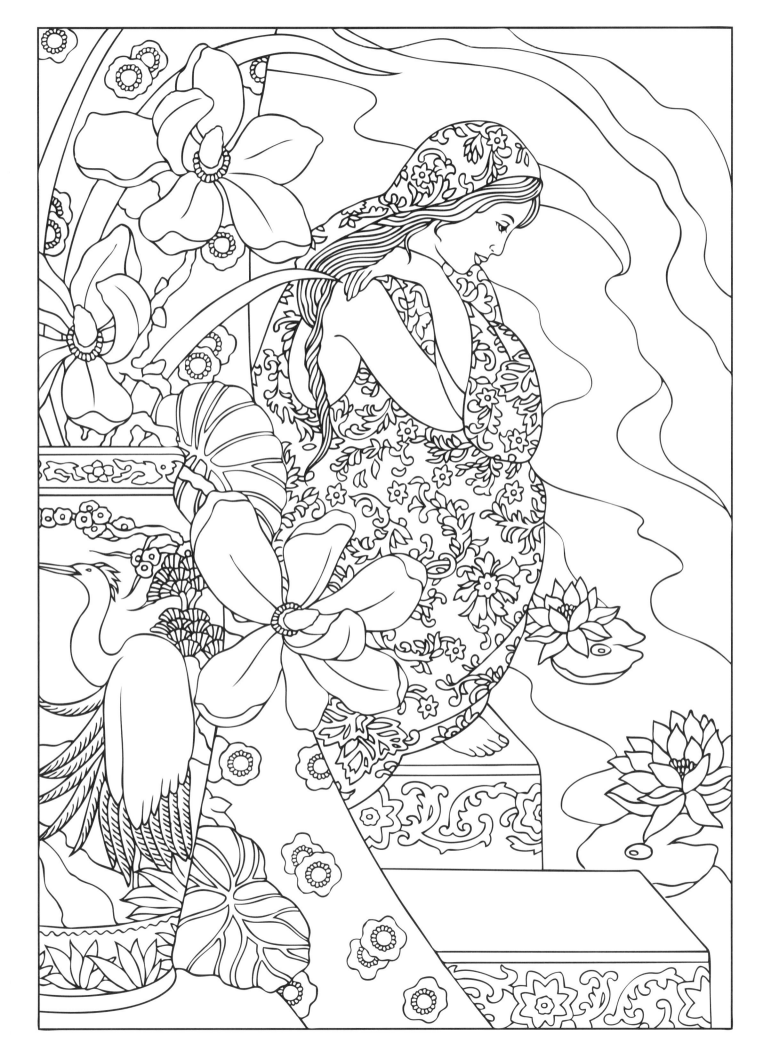

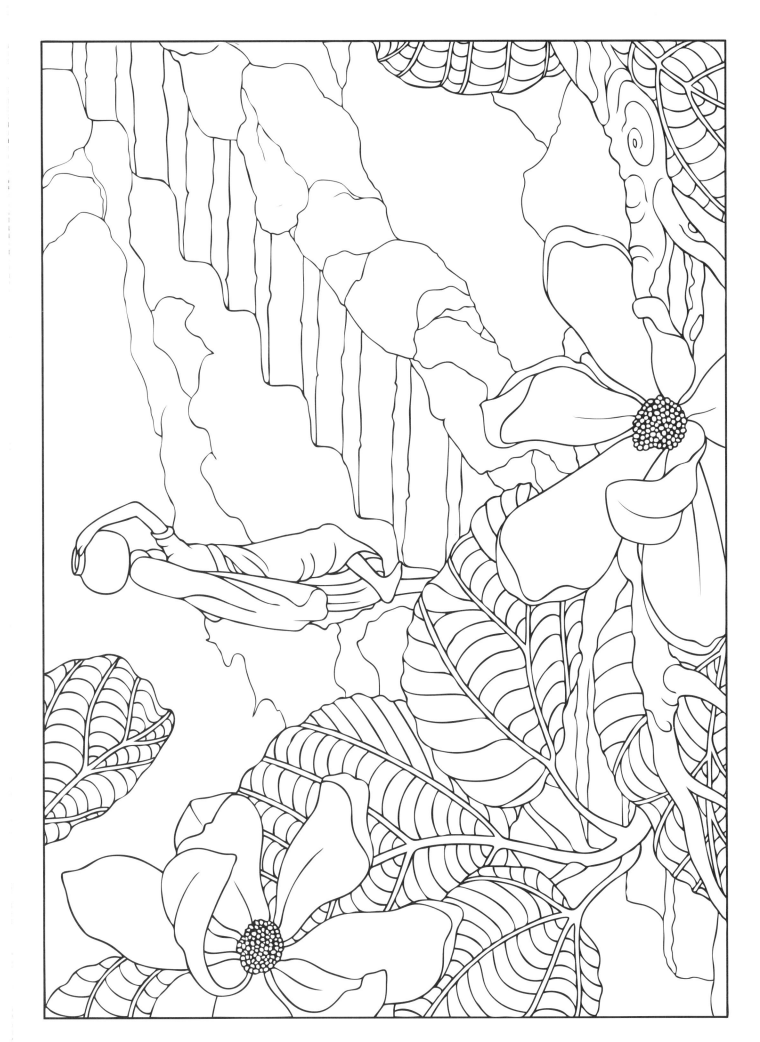

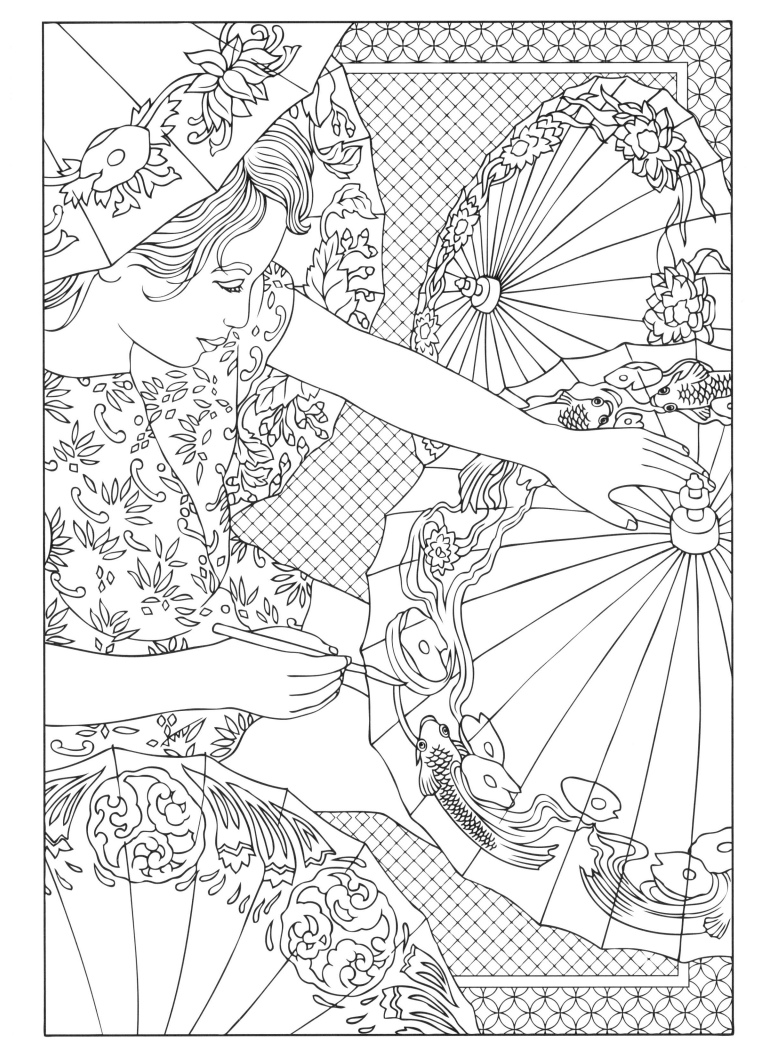

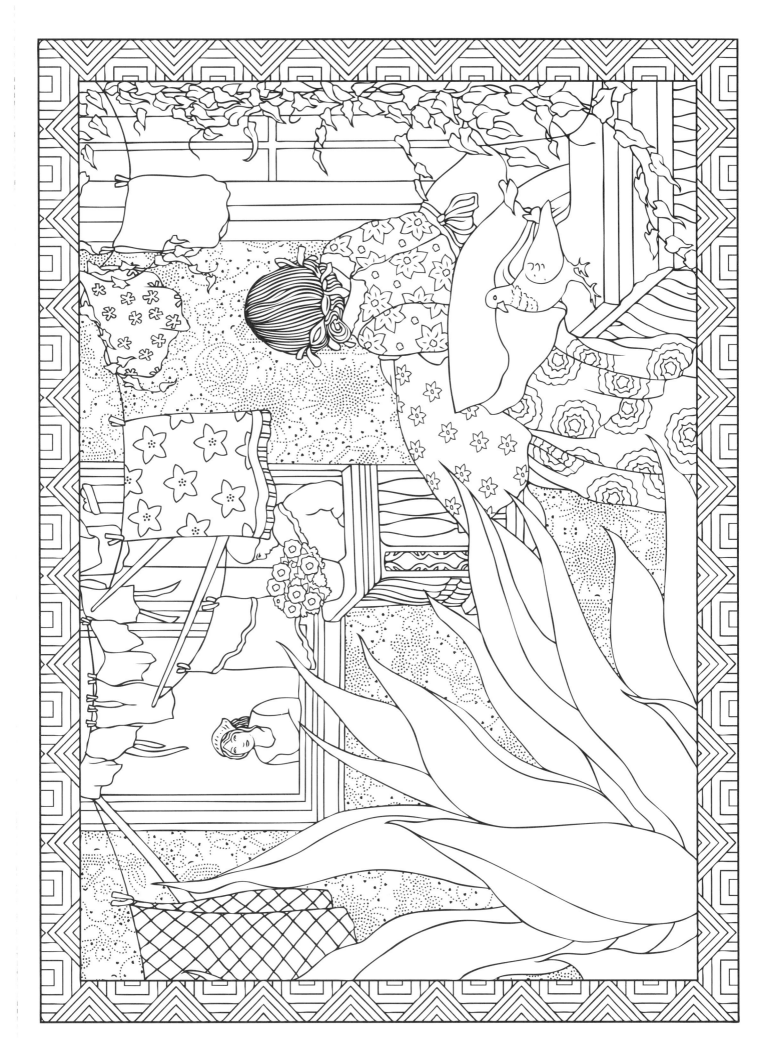

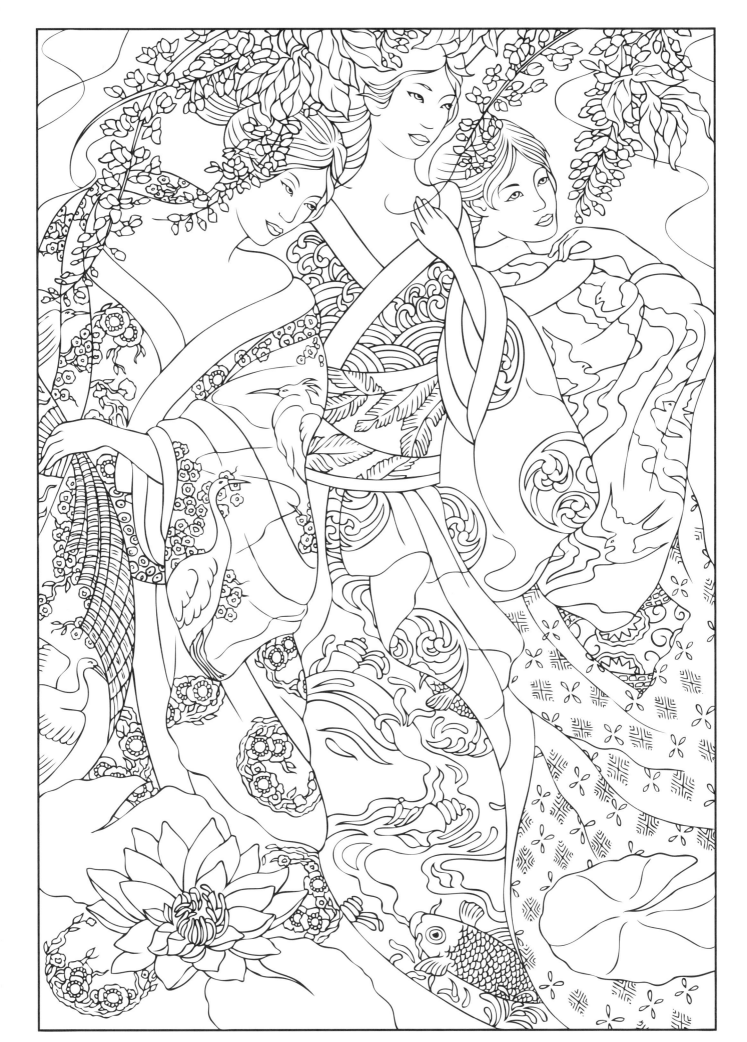

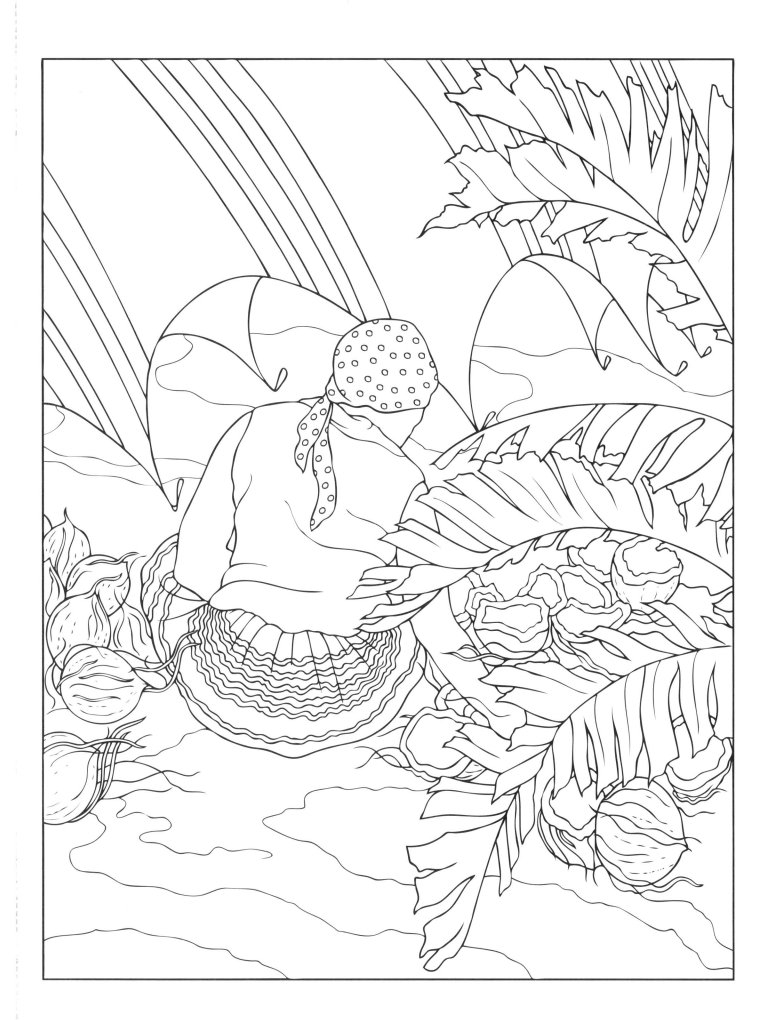

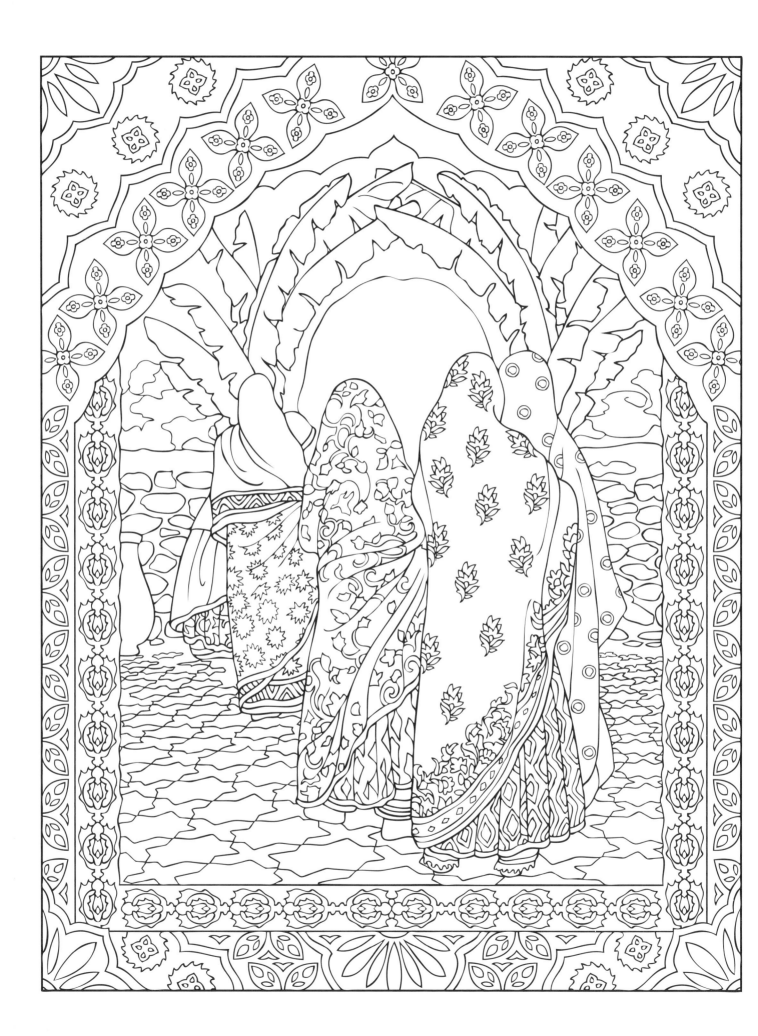

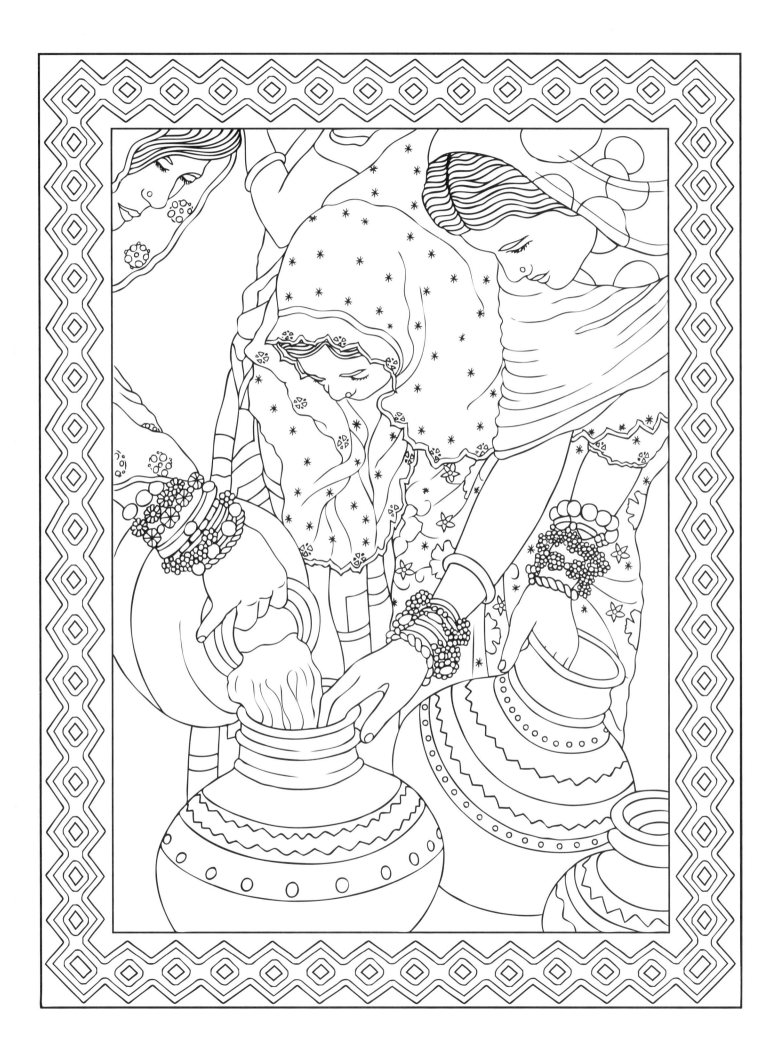

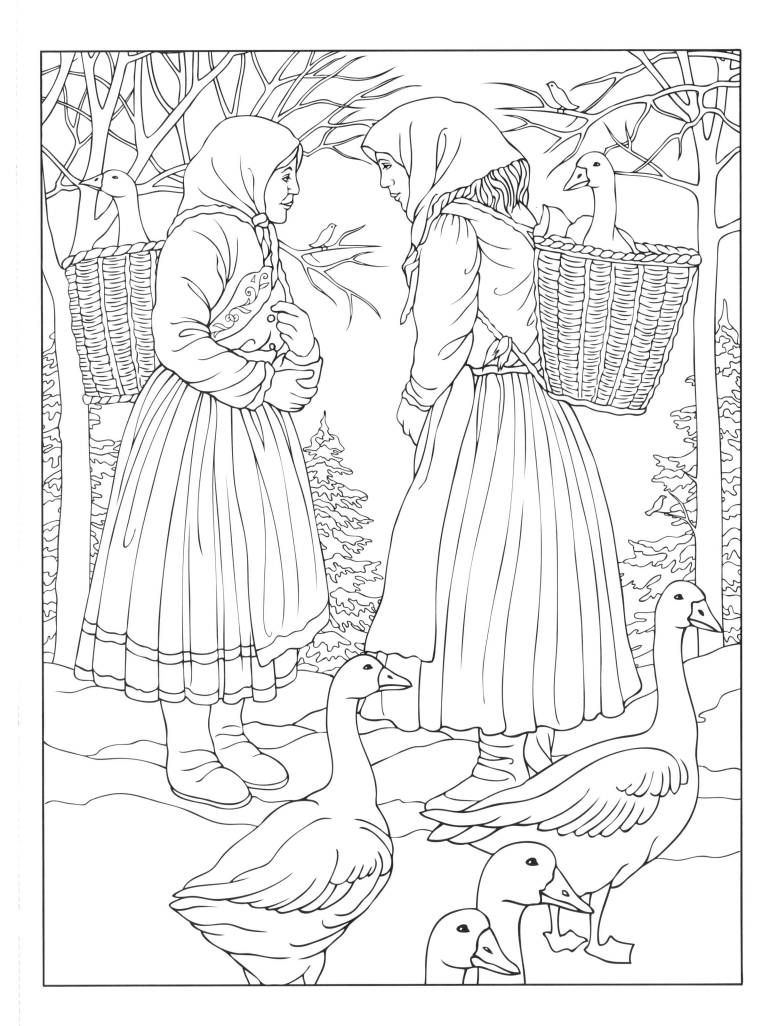

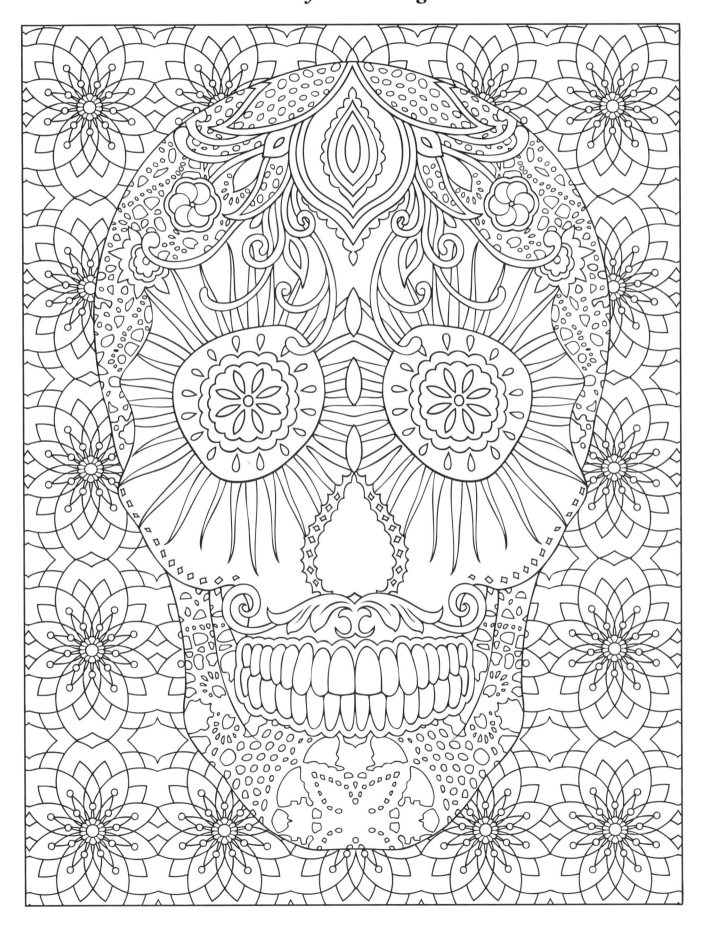

Color Bars

Use these bars to test your coloring medium and palette. Don't be afraid to try unique color combinations!

Color Bars

Use these bars to test your coloring medium and palette. Don't be afraid to try unique color combinations!

Color Bars

Use these bars to test your coloring medium and palette. Don't be afraid to try unique color combinations!

Our vast, diverse, and multicultural world is colorful beyond our imagination. There are an estimated 8,000 different cultural groups in the world, and that's just only those that have been counted. Culture consists of many elements, such as a people group's history, language, art, and cuisine, just to name a few. Only 4.4 percent of the entire world population lives in the United States, which itself is a kaleidoscope of many different ethnic groups.

Marty Noble's Peaceful World brings together the art, clothing, commerce, flora and fauna, everyday scenes, and myths from countries such as China, Japan, India, Indonesia, Guatemala, Morocco, Italy, Thailand, Mexico, and Turkey. These interweaving tapestries from distinct communities come together in a harmony of line and color, forming the single human race. With a deeper understanding of both the similarities and differences among us, we can come closer to the goal of world peace and share the experiences of our common humanity.

❧

Marty Noble is a *New York Times'* bestselling coloring book artist, with more than 300 books published and over 3 million copies of her books sold. Marty was raised in Santa Barbara by a family of artists. She pursued her creative interests from an early age with the traditional Indonesian batik wax-resist dyeing technique. Her work grew from simple pieces to extremely detailed paintings that earned her a reputation in galleries, where they were sold for a period of twenty years. In the seventies, Marty switched to watercolor illustration and her art has been used in books, posters, puzzles, greeting cards, plate designs, and calendars. One of Marty's favorite subjects is illustrating the cultures of peoples from all over the world, which stems from her travels to South America, Europe, the Middle East, and Southeast Asia. Today, Marty lives in Santa Barbara, California, where she finds continual inspiration for her current series of photo art prints that depict the natural beauty of Southern California.

Marty Noble's Sugar Skulls is available wherever books are sold.

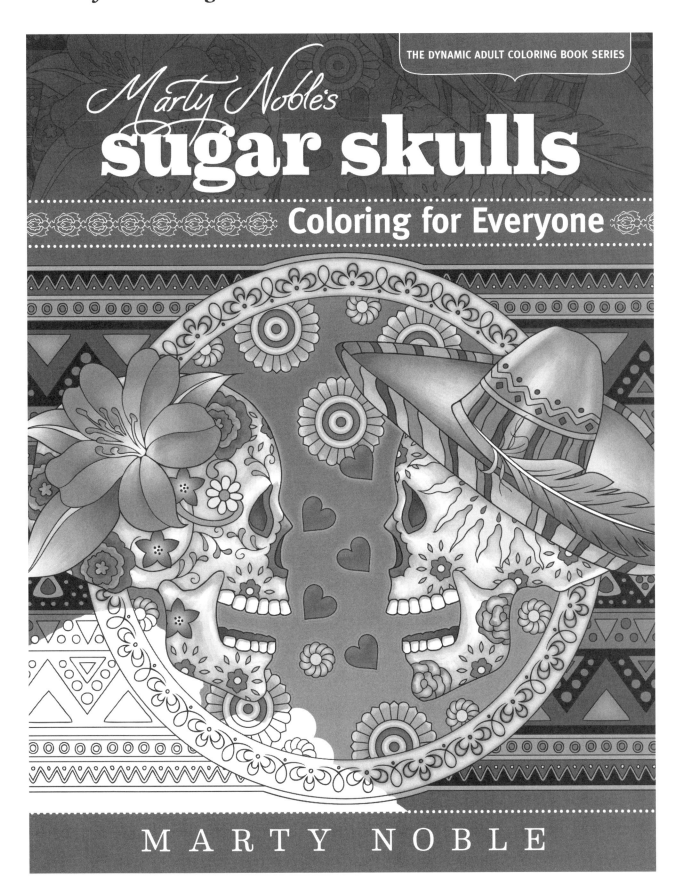

Also Available from Skyhorse Publishing

Creative Stress Relieving Adult Coloring Book Series

Art Nouveau: Coloring for Artists

Art Nouveau: Coloring for Everyone

Butterfly Gardens: Coloring for Everyone

Curious Cats and Kittens: Coloring for Artists

Curious Cats and Kittens: Coloring for Everyone

Exotic Chickens: Coloring for Everyone

Mandalas: Coloring for Artists

Mandalas: Coloring for Everyone

Mehndi: Coloring for Artists

Mehndi: Coloring for Everyone

Nature's Wonders: Coloring for Everyone

Nirvana: Coloring for Artists

Nirvana: Coloring for Everyone

Paisleys: Coloring for Artists

Paisleys: Coloring for Everyone

Tapestries, Fabrics, and Quilts: Coloring for Artists

Tapestries, Fabrics, and Quilts: Coloring for Everyone

Whimsical Designs: Coloring for Artists

Whimsical Designs: Coloring for Everyone

Whimsical Woodland Creatures: Coloring for Artists

Whimsical Woodland Creatures: Coloring for Everyone

Zen Patterns and Designs: Coloring for Artists

Zen Patterns and Designs: Coloring for Everyone

The Peaceful Adult Coloring Book Series

Adult Coloring Book: Be Inspired

Adult Coloring Book: De-Stress

Adult Coloring Book: Keep Calm

Adult Coloring Book: Relax

Portable Coloring for Creative Adults

Calming Patterns: Portable Coloring for Creative Adults

Flying Wonders: Portable Coloring for Creative Adults

Natural Wonders: Portable Coloring for Creative Adults

Sea Life: Portable Coloring for Creative Adults

On-the-Go Adult Coloring Books

Creative Mindfulness: A Forest of Tranquility

Creative Mindfulness: Peaceful Designs